# A Salute
# to Service

## The Rebirth of Patriotism

## Mike Radford

New Leaf Press

New Leaf Press edition

First printing: July 2004

ISBN: 0-89221-597-6

Library of Congress Number: 2004106966

**Printed in the United States of America**

Please visit our website for other great titles:
www.newleafpress.net

For information regarding author interviews,
please contact the publicity department at (870) 438-5288.

## Dedicated to the "Captain" — Timmy Rogers

My brother, my best friend,
and the greatest man I ever knew!

If you met Timmy, you were blessed. He was a Vietnam hero of the highest order, and his impact on my life immeasurable. They say you can judge a man by the number of friends he has when he dies. Timmy went "home" on Monday, May 17, 2004, at 7:15 a.m. Then on May 20, he looked down from heaven to see nearly 2,000 men, women, and children gathered to celebrate his life.

Timmy used to say, "Mikey, you are my hero; you've *done* everything I ever wanted to do in my life." To that I would respond, "And Timmy, you *are* everything I've ever wanted to *be* in my life."

My wife, Shari, was his "sister" in Christian love, and our hearts are filled with Timmy's spirit and wonderful memories of great joy for having him in our lives.

*Gayle Kirchner, Mike, Shari, and Tim*

"The United States of America will be a better place if everyone reads this book. I highly recommend it."

Jack LaLanne
Fitness expert; WWII veteran

"If you are a parent who believes in God, family, and America, get this book for your kids!"

Dr. Joe White
President, Kanakuk Kamps

"Please accept my most wholehearted thanks and admiration for all the work you are doing to inspire patriotism in this great nation of ours."

Senator Kit Bond
Missouri

"My mom and dad believed in everything that Mike writes about in this book. I recommend you buy it and read it to your little ones tonight."

Roy Rogers Jr.

"We attend the same church. We believe in the same God, and now you can experience Mike's ability to recharge your patriotic batteries. He's the best at what he does."

Dr. Gary Smalley

# Two Special Thank Yous

Nearly 15 years ago, God blessed me. It happened at a time when I thought single parenthood and loneliness were my destiny. After much prayer, in fact, very specific prayer, God brought a woman into my life who has become best friend, business partner, and my wife — Shari Ann. She continues to amaze me with her joyful and happy spirit. Her charming ways and spontaneous laughter enchant all who meet her. My wish is that every husband and wife be blessed with an adoring partner, because life is a ball when you are in love.

The second "thank you" I wish to make is to everyone who encouraged me to write this book, especially the ones who took the time to write and share stories of their family heroes. We are blessed to live in the United States of America, and it is our duty to pass along the legacy of service to country. Whether you or yours served in the military, law enforcement, or rescue and fire departments, this book is my salute to your service.

# Contents

# Foreword
## by Regis Philbin

For a decade in Branson, Missouri, Mike has lead the way celebrating and honoring our servicemen and servicewomen. Joy and I believe this book will further our founders' vision of God, family, and country. If you love this nation, pass this book on to every young person in your family. We need a rebirth of patriotism and old-fashioned American values.

On my last day in the navy, I went to say goodbye to a tough marine major named Kiegler Flake, who asked me what I was going to do with my life. When I told him I was thinking of trying to get into TV but didn't know if I had the talent, he got in my face and shouted, "Don't you know you can have anything in this life? Now do you want it?!" I screamed back, "Yes, sir!" and moved out to Hollywood the next day. I hope this book will inspire you in the same way and you will pursue your "American Dream."

# Introduction

## The Angel on the Highway

It all began as I drove along I-94 returning from a speaking engagement at the capitol in Madison, Wisconsin. I noticed a van ahead of me in the slow lane. As I drew closer, I could see words on the spare tire cover attached to the back of the vehicle. As I read the words, goose bumps tightened on my skin: "The men and women who served and died for our country must NEVER be forgotten."

Chills began to crawl up my back. I pushed on the accelerator and pulled alongside the driver's door. An elderly man sat behind the wheel . . . obviously a veteran. I smiled and gave a thumbs-up gesture and began to pull ahead. Suddenly the old man began honking his horn, accelerating, until our cars were once again side by side.

What happened next was the turning point, the exact moment that changed my life forever. The white-haired veteran rolled down his window, stuck his arm out, pointed toward heaven then covered his heart and pointed directly back at me. At that moment I knew I had to create a show that would honor his generation, the generation that literally saved the world during WWII.

Over the past nine and one-half years in Branson, dozens of pastors, priests, and rabbis have seen my show or heard me speak of this experience. All agree that no one has seen this van or the white-haired man. They say it was an angel put there to inspire me to spread old-fashioned patriotism honoring God, family, and country. And now, you too have been called to join the battle of good over evil.

Bear in mind, my foremost objective throughout this book is to inspire you — to light a fire inside your heart that will motivate you to want to make your town a better place. I want you to look deep inside and find the roots of your patriotism, to discover hidden passions that will help propel you to a higher level of commitment to God, family, and country.

Enjoy the patriotic journey you are about to take. Share the inspiration with those you love, and together we will chart a new course for America. Together we can make a difference.

# The Hall of Heroes

They say when a concept is ready, it's referred to as "an idea whose time has come." And so it was in 1995 when our "Remember When Show" began receiving not only kudos and accolades, but countless family memorabilia and pieces of military history. The depth to which we connected with folks surprised Shari and me. After all, we were just two entertainers trying to add joy, laughter, music, and patriotism to the hearts of those who came. There was no way we could forecast how deep our connections actually were.

In the early days of our Branson experience, we often played to small crowds, but the size of the audience really didn't matter. The manner in which our show unfolded was not just entertainment; we transported them to their childhood days, times when men lined up at recruiting offices from coast to coast. These were the positive role models of the era. Another aspect of those times was the passion with which American citizens displayed their patriotism and demonstrated unlimited allegiance to fighting evil.

And so began the collection of military medals, uniforms, and memorabilia of times past. It became a weekly experience, not knowing from where or whom the next "treasure" would arrive, but they always came. One of the first priceless moments occurred when we had just finished building our very own theater room inside Branson's IMAX Complex. One of the construction workers came up to us one day and offered a gift, his contribution to the display we lovingly called, "Grandma's Attic." I can still see this aging couple holding out the small case, "Here," he said, "this needs to be a part of your display." We looked into his aging eyes and witnessed the tears. Shari reached out, taking the case. A slight smile creased the corner of the man's lips. "Go ahead, open it," he said. Shari cradled the case gently in her hands, opening it with the respect the moment demanded.

Inside the old leather case was a Purple Heart, the same as first given by General George Washington during the War of Independence.

Shari looked up quickly and said, "We can't accept this! It belongs in your family!" The older couple gently touched her shoulder and explained they were the only ones who remembered their young uncle who had marched off to fight communism in Korea. He was just a boy, 21 in 1952, who answered the call to serve. James F. Lowe, a young lad from Missouri went off to war, never to be seen again.

The lady said, "We're the only ones left who knew Uncle Jim and this is the best way we could think of to honor his memory."

Since that day, literally thousands of pieces of military memorabilia and photographs have been placed in our "Hall of Heroes." What be-

*Purple Heart earned by James F. Lowe*

gan as a simple display has evolved into one of the largest tributes to the men and women who served in the United States Armed Forces. The original Hall is still standing inside Branson's IMAX, but nearly every square inch of wall space is covered.

In 2000, Bill Weimar, the director of marketing for the Radisson Hotel in Branson, liked our idea and invited us to create an even larger patriotic display. General manager Tammy Johnson agreed. In the four years since Attorney General John Ashcroft cut the ceremonial grand opening ribbon, nearly 900 feet of wall space has been decorated. The drama of the second "Hall of Heroes" can be felt the moment

*Mike and Shari with Attorney General John Ashcroft*

you begin to gaze upon the thousands of faces framed under glass. It's a place of pilgrimage, and a living scrapbook of America's youth from the time of Lincoln right up to the faces of kids who liberated Iraq.

Huge shadowbox cases are filled with GI Joe's uniforms worn on Iwo Jima and a bronze statue of the celebrated flag-raising given to us by Austin Ring, one of the Marines who survived the battle. WACs and WAVEs are remembered too, as is "Rosie-the-Riveter." Another shows a sailor's whites worn on December 7th, 1941, at Pearl Harbor, the sweat stains still visibly imprinted into the fabric. One dramatic display shows a piece of barbed wire from the infamous Nazi prison camp Stalag 17 — donated by Charlie Siebert. Down the hall you'll see a tribute to the Korean and Vietnam veterans, and another for the VUMS (Veterans of Underage Military Service), some of whom were children 12 years old at the time who lied about their age so they could serve in WWII. Cold War tributes, peace-timers too. None are left out, not even the men and women who serve "on the home front" protecting Americans — law enforcement, firefighters, and rescue personnel.

Large colorful maps of Vietnam and Korea are nearly invisible as countless visitors added their signatures — reconnecting with their fellow comrades of those wars. A complete area gives honor to every F.B.I. agent who fell in the line of duty — the only display of its kind outside of F.B.I. headquarters in Washington, D.C. There are flags which covered a fallen hero's coffin, and unit flags from outfits around the world — the Flying Tigers, the Chosen Few, Pearl Harbor survivors, and countless others.

Our hope is that every city will follow our lead and create their own "living" tribute to the kids who served from their area. Maybe you are the one we are looking for to lead the cause. These Halls of Heroes are priceless in their impact and vital in teaching our nation's youth about the sacrifices their families and neighbors made so they may live in freedom. It cannot be said enough, "Freedom is NOT free." Schools can have field trips where children can see with their own eyes the faces of the men and women who came before them, the ones who teach what patriotism is really about. It's vital that we pass the values upon which our republic was founded: God, family, and country. So if you would like to create a dynamic attraction to your area, all it requires is one businessman or woman to step forward and say, "Yes, it *is* time we say thank you."

## To Those Who Led . . . For Those Who Follow

The Hall of Heroes concept is one that can be done in every town, large or small, across the United States. Each town's Hall of Heroes would be as unique as the collection of veterans and active military personnel from their individual communities. It is a project that could combine the efforts of area schools, families, libraries, veterans and businesses.

One of the most poignant displays in the Branson Hall of Heroes honors servicemen who signed up when they were underage; another section honors all of the Congressional Medal of Honor recipients. While these are examples which are now unique to this Hall of Heroes, other special displays around the country could focus on women in the service, minorities who served, and even unique medal recipients — the possibilities are virtually endless. Or they can serve as a general collection featuring every man and woman who has served in the past or is on active duty now — including reservist and National Guard units.

**Honoring Your Veteran or Active-Duty Military Family Member in Ten Easy Steps:**

1. Gather up photos of your veteran and military family member in uniform.

2. Type or write the name, unit information, and other relevant information you already know about this person on a piece of paper.

3. Be sure to make note of any special commendations or medals.

4. Take your photos to a photo copy service and make copies of your original photos.

5. Frame your photo or photos (with or without matting — matting does give you the opportunity to do additional decoration or add writing to the photo display).

6. Write a letter to your veteran or, if deceased, get in contact with older family members or someone else who might have known that person well to verify the information you already know and gather additional information.

7. Interview this person briefly — by phone, on audio cassette or video, or even by e-mail if available — about his military service or the service of the deceased veteran.

(These are invaluable archives for your family and for future generations during genealogical searches.)

8. Other sources of information on your veteran can be found in heritage centers or through contacting federal and state resources which contain archive information on veterans. If you know a special date of service, or even to find the obituary of a deceased veteran, don't forget to contact your local newspaper to see what they have in their archives (often photocopies or back issues are available for little or no fees). Also, information can be obtained through the individual unit histories and ongoing reunions of various veterans groups.

9. You could also create a special family scrapbook — featuring the history of military service in your family through the different generations, or you could focus smaller scrapbooks on individual service members or family veterans.

10. Make contact with the local veterans organizations in your community — see what projects or efforts they have underway to honor veterans.

## Educational Partnership Opportunities

1. Can be used as a class project or schoolwide activity (flyer mailout to reach relevant school personnel).

2. Can be used to teach library research and writing skills, and can be used as a tie-in for history and current events.

3. Area schools which may have adopted active service personnel in Afghanistan or Iraq, or area national guardsmen.

4. Brings history alive for younger generations — within a national context and as an addition to their own family history.

5.  Media classes could participate in filming or audio recording interviews of area veterans, which could create a multimedia section for their Hall of Heroes. (Copies could then be sent to the Library of Congress for their Veterans History Project, a special effort to preserve the rich military history of service to our country.)

## Supplies List

- Framing and matting supplies and photo albums
- Film
- Audio and video cassettes (for local participation in the Library of Congress Veterans History Project or for your own archives)
- Glue, tape, and other supplies
- Scrapbooks and assorted scrapbook supplies (stickers, paper, etc.)

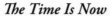

*The Time Is Now*

*Mike's "Hall of Heroes" inside the Radisson Hotel in Branson, Missouri*

# A Wake Up Call

We are in a war, a battle for the very survival of the United States of America. This battle is very different from the atrocities of 9-11-01. This is a conflict of idealogy that is silent and unrecognized by most Americans. A war that, if lost, will see the sovereignty of our nation handed to people who are secretly maneuvering to place our country under the control of the "global village," or as others call it, the United Nations.

Our founders never intended for our sons and daughters to fight or be peacekeepers under the control of foreign governments. That is NOT what United States sovereignty means, and when a soldier is commanded to take action from officers of foreign armies, it flies in the face of the military pledge of defending our nation against all enemies, foreign and domestic. If we surrender our sovereignty, freedom, and control to foreign military powers, we, in our lifetime, will watch as our sons and daughters continue to die under UN flags in battles around the world. What will we tell their widows and children? Will it be enough to say their daddy or mommy died protecting a piece of land that has been the scene of ethnic cleansing for thousands of years? Will they understand why our nation sent them to some far-off land to die, defending causes we know nothing about? There is only one way for God-loving men and women to prevent this careless absurdity from taking place. We must become reborn in the passionate belief that we are Americans, "one nation under God," and will not waiver from the ideals our founding fathers set forth in our Bill of Rights and the Constitution of the United States. We are liberators, not conquerors.

One of the things I want this book to accomplish is to renew your sense of American pride, because with a renewed sense of who we are comes a rebirth of those values most Americans hold dear. It is critically important we do this and teach our youngsters that living in the United States of America is a God-given privilege, not just a birthright. We cannot take for granted or assume that the blessings of liberty will automatically be transferred from one generation to the next. We must teach our children and grandchildren the price others have paid so they can enjoy gifts of liberty and the true meaning of freedom that we have in our country today.

Too many of us have forgotten there are over 8,200 servicemen MIA (missing in action) in Korea, and nearly 3,000 in Vietnam. We must not forget them! Don't wait until Veterans Day, the 4th of July, or Memorial Day to think of these abandoned patriots. When you see a veteran who was lucky enough to come home, shake his hand. Thank him for serving our country to keep our republic free. This gesture will be something he never expected and the reaction will be something you will never forget. No, freedom is not free. As the Ambassador of Patriotism I now appoint you as Deputy Ambassadors. America needs you to help keep this renewed spirit alive. Don't let the flame die out — otherwise the terrorists will laugh at our lack of resolve.

# 9-11-01 — The Day America Changed Forever

It felt like a bad dream, a nightmare . . . a scary movie. But we all knew it was real. We sat on couches and carpet, we leaned against each other and watched in horror as tears fell like rain and our hearts ached as one. In my mind I kept asking, "When is Bruce Willis's character going to appear?" "Where is Arnold Schwartzeneggar, the Terminator?" Watching the planes hit the towers seemed like special effects on a Hollywood soundstage. People worldwide were in a hypnotic daze as we watched the most evil act in the history of our blessed homeland.

Those of us who were born after WWII could only imagine what it was like for the men and women who were at Pearl Harbor when the Japanese attacked on December 7, 1941. I can remember my mother telling me of the uncles and friends who were killed that day, never realizing how truly heartbroken our nation was during those days. I do now.

Many years ago I was a flight instructor in one of Florida's international flight schools. Two of my students were Muslim fundamentalists and seemed like polite young men and excellent pilots. Back in the '70s there were thousands of foreign student pilots training in the USA. It was big business, huge business, and yes, they usually had lots of cash. Without giving their names, for obvious reasons, let me just say these guys scared me. One of my students looked me in the eye one day and said, "Don't you ever betray me because I will kill you like a jackal." His black eyes burned into mine. He scared me a lot! Now after watching their "brothers" murder thousands of innocent people, I realize I had good reason to fear them. These folks aren't like you and me. They are different and scary in their fanatical beliefs.

The events of 9-11 *are* another Pearl Harbor, and, like the attack in 1941, this too has awakened the sleeping giant. Young Americans flocked to recruiting stations to join the cause. What does that say about our kids? It says today's young citizens are as patriotic as those of any era before them. It says they, too, stand tall for ALL the right reasons.

The goal of the evil ones was to slaughter Americans, but also to kill our spirit. But they got a surprise, didn't they? The terrorists saw something they never expected. Once again, we've become The UNITED States of America — "One Nation Under God," indivisible, meaning NO ONE can divide us. We cherish life, liberty, and the pursuit of happiness. It's our heritage, our God-given right under the Constitution. They indeed

*Patriotism past . . . and reborn*

have awakened this sleeping giant and the world will see America rebuild its skyscrapers, and in time our hearts will heal. But we will never forget, or find ourselves slumbering while the enemy sneaks inside the gate.

We must remember too that these evil ones do not represent their entire culture. Millions of their ethnic brothers and sisters live in peace as God-fearing Americans. That diversity of gender and bloodline is what makes "Americans." We are the world's great melting pot, created from every human bloodline on earth. Think how unique we are . . . if your heritage is European, you are an American. If your ancestors came from Norway, you are an American. If you have no idea where your family's roots originate, you are still an American — unique from every nation in the world. It is our diversified society that makes us truly different from all other nations — a fact about our society that should be celebrated because it's the diversity itself that created our greatness.

The late Dale Evans wrote a song every child loves: "Red and yellow, black and white, we are precious in His sight — Jesus loves the little children of the world." Roy Rogers and Dale Evans proved "good-guys" can achieve greatness. They were the "American Dream."

And while on the subject of greatness, the Merchant Marines were true heroes during WWII. I hope you will always remember the men and women who served, and the thousands who gave up every tomorrow for you and me. The WWII generation literally saved the world when they were called to serve. Most people today look at these patriots as simply somebody's grandmother or grandfather. But when they were kids back in the '40s, they had to march, sail, or fly into hell to save the world for our generation. "Thanks" is not enough, because we owe them so much more.

To those who served in the Korean War, know too that yours is NOT the forgotten war. We will always remember you and the great sacrifices you gave blocking the spread of communism. And to the Vietnam veteran — you are so special and deserve so much more respect than you received back in the '60s and '70s. It's long overdue, but please accept this heartfelt sentiment: "Welcome home!" My prayer is that you can find the strength inside to "leave it over there." Those of you who served but were lucky to avoid combat, you too are deserving of our gratitude. It was just luck that kept you from harm's way. Maybe you are a peacetime vet, or you served in the guard or reserves. You are no less a veteran than the kid who fell at Gettysburg, Grenada, Da Nang, Desert Storm, or in our current fight against evil. You answered the call and we are forever grateful.

That brings me to our last group of patriots — the men and women who put on the uniforms of firefighter, police officer, or EMT personnel. Their response on 9-11-01 was heroism of the highest order. To enter buildings they knew were coming down . . . they rescued thousands of terrified souls from around the world. Their actions were service above self.

And we will never forget the heroes aboard the United Airlines jet over Pennsylvania. We will forever honor the courage of Todd Beamer, 32, from Cranbury, New Jersey. He said, "Let's roll!" preserving the Capitol or the White House — most believe those were the next targets. The other amazing heroes on board who demonstrated true American courage were Alan Beaven, 48, from Oakland, California; Mark Bingham, 31, from San Francisco; Thomas Burnett Jr., 38, from San Ramon, California; and Jeremy Glick, 31, from West Milford, New Jersey. America will never be the same. That day was the turning point. All Americans again realize that freedom is not free. We will forever defend "life, liberty, and the pursuit of happiness." And we will always remember 9-11-01.

# SECTION ONE

## *"Over There"*

# *The American GI*

When I was still a little kid, my grandma Harriet loved taking me to watch parades. Grandma looked forward to standing along the curb with her little "Mikey." I remember vividly seeing all the veterans marching, their heads held high. I'd watch Grandma's eyes fill with tears, then fall across her rosy cheeks as the boys marched down Main Street carrying flags and rifles. Patriotism was big back then.

*Dennis K. Showers, Mike's best friend, killed in Vietnam.*

"Why are you crying?" I asked my grandma. "I'm proud of our boys, Mikey, I'm so proud of our boys," she'd say. Now 40-odd years later her voice rings loud in my heart. I'm proud of "our boys," too. Isn't it time for kids today to learn and feel that old-fashioned pride and to discover the GI and learn of the sacrifices and heroics they displayed during the days of their youth? The American GI has become an unsung hero in our time and now,

★ ★ ★ 26 ★ ★ ★

because of recent events, our nation has turned back toward old values and we are once again saluting the countless contributions our G.I.'s give to preserve our way of life.

In 1999, *Time* magazine prepared a list of the ten most influential people of the last century. They named "the American GI" the most influential "person" of the 21st century. When the honor was announced, General Colin Powell gave the introduction to the award:

> As chairman of the Joint Chiefs of Staff, I referred to the men and women of the armed forces as "GIs." It got me in trouble with some of my colleagues at the time. Several years earlier, the army had officially excised the term as an unfavorable character-ization derived from the designation "government issue." Sailors and marines wanted to be known as sailors and marines. Airmen, notwithstanding their origins as a rib of the army, wished to be called, simply, "airmen." Collectively, they were blandly referred to as "service members."
>
> I persisted in using "GIs" and found I was in good com-pany. Newspapers and television shows used it all the time. The most famous and successful government education program was known as the GI Bill, and it still uses that title for a newer gen-eration of veterans. When you added one of the most common boys' names to it, you got GI Joe, and the name of the most popular boy's toy ever, the GI Joe action figure. And let's not forget GI Jane.
>
> GI is a World War II term that two generations later contin-ues to conjure up the warmest and proudest memories of a noble war that pitted pure good against pure evil, and good triumphed.

The victors in that war were the American GIs, the Lillies and Joes, the farmer from Iowa and the steelworker from Pittsburgh, who stepped off a landing craft into the hell of Omaha Beach. The GI was the wisecracking kid marine from Brooklyn who clawed his way up a deadly hill on a Pacific island.

He was a black fighter pilot escorting white bomber pilots over Italy and Germany, proving that skin color had nothing to do with skill or courage. He was a native Japanese-American infantryman released from his own country's concentration camp to join the fight. She was a nurse relieving the agony of a dying teenager. He was a landing signal officer standing on the edge of a heaving aircraft carrier with two signal paddles in his hands, helping guide a dive-bomber pilot back onto the deck. They were America.

They reflected our diverse origins. They were the embodiment of the American spirit of courage and dedication. They were truly a "people's army," going forth on a crusade to save democracy and freedom, to defeat tyrants, to save oppressed peoples and to make their families proud of them. They were the Private Ryans, and they stood firm in the thin red line.

For most of those GIs, World War II was the adventure of their lifetime. Nothing they would ever do in the future would match their experiences as the warriors of democracy, saving the world from its own insanity. You can still see them in every Fourth of July color guard, their gait faltering but ever proud.

Their forebearers went by other names: doughboys, Yanks, buffalo soldiers, Johnny Reb, Rough Riders. But "GI" will be forever lodged in the consciousness of our nation to apply to all of them. The GI carried the value system of the American people. The GIs were the surest guarantee of America's commitment.

For more than 200 years, they answered the call to fight the nation's battles. They never went forth as mercenaries on the road to conquest. They went forth as reluctant warriors, as citizen soldiers. They were as gentle in victory as they were vicious in battle.

I've had survivors of Nazi concentration camps tell me of the joy they experienced as the GIs liberated them: America had arrived!

I've had a wealthy Japanese businessman come into my office and tell me what it was like for him as a child in 1945 to await the arrival of the dreaded American beasts, and instead meet a smiling GI who gave him a Hershey bar. In thanks, the businessman was donating a large sum of money to the USO.

Photo courtesy of Plumlee Photography, Oak Grove, AR

*An evening with General Colin Powell at the College of the Ozarks*

After thanking him, I gave him as a souvenir a Hershey bar I had autographed. He took it and began to cry. The 20th century can be called many things, but it was most certainly a century of war. The American GIs helped defeat fascism and communism.

They came home in triumph from the ferocious battlefields of World Wars I and II. In Korea and Vietnam they fought just as bravely as their predecessors, but no triumphant receptions awaited them at home. They soldiered on through the twilight struggles of the cold war and showed what they were capable of in Desert Storm. The American people took them into their hearts again.

In this century, hundreds of thousands of GIs died to bring to the beginning of the 21st century the victory of democracy as the ascendant political system on the face of the earth. The GIs were willing to travel far away and give their lives, if necessary, to secure the rights and freedoms of others. Only a nation such as ours, based on a firm moral foundation, could make such a request of its citizens. And the GIs wanted nothing more than to get the job done and then return home safely. All they asked for in repayment from those they freed was the opportunity to help them become part of the world of democracy — and just enough land to bury their fallen comrades beneath simple white crosses and Stars of David.

The volunteer GIs of today stand watch in Korea, the Persian Gulf, Europe, and the dangerous terrain of the Balkans. We must never see them as mere hirelings, off in a corner of our society. They are our best, and we owe them our full support and our sincerest thanks. As this century closes, we look back to identify the great leaders and personalities of the past 100 years. We do so in a world still troubled, but full of promise. That promise was gained by the young men and women of America who fought and died for freedom. Near the top of any listing of the most important people of the 20th century must stand, in singular honor, the American GI[1]

General Colin Powell, former chairman of the Joint Chiefs of Staff, is now leading our battle against enemies foreign and domestic. As our secretary of state, his work is literally protecting our lives, our fortunes, and our sacred honor. Pray that God will give him wisdom and guidance in these troubled times in which we live. We need His hand to be upon our nation's leaders to guide them with invisible wisdom and the blessings to keep us free from evil.

*103-year-young Charles Buckner, WWI & WWII veteran*

# *Judge Me by My Footsteps*

### Author unknown

*God bless our nation's disabled veterans! I'd like to share this next story about a soldier who was finally coming home after having fought in Vietnam. I don't remember who sent me the following story, but when I finished reading it, I was in tears.*

He called his parents from San Francisco. "Mom and Dad, I'm coming home, but I've got a favor to ask. I have a friend I'd like to bring with me."

"Sure," they replied, "we'd love to meet him."

"There's something you should know," the son continued. "He was hurt pretty badly in the fighting. He stepped on a land mine and lost an arm and a leg. He has nowhere else to go, and I want him to come live with us."

"I'm sorry to hear that, son. Maybe we can help him find somewhere to live."

"No, Mom and Dad, I want him to live with us."

"Son," said the father, "you don't know what you're asking. Someone with such a handicap would be a terrible burden on us. We have our own lives to live, and we can't let something like this interfere with our lives. I think you should just come home and forget about this guy. He'll find a way to live on his own."

At that point, the son hung up the phone. The parents heard nothing more from him. A few days later, however, they received a call from the San Francisco police. They were told their son had died after falling from a building. The police believed it was suicide. The grief-stricken parents flew to San Francisco and were taken to the city morgue to identify the body of their son. They recognized him, but to their horror they also discovered something they didn't know — their son had only one arm and one leg.

The parents in this story are like many of us. We find it easy to love those who are good-looking or fun to have around, but we don't like people who inconvenience us or make us feel uncomfortable. We would rather stay away from people who aren't as healthy, beautiful, or smart as we are. Thankfully, there's someone who won't treat us that way. Someone who loves us with an unconditional love that welcomes us into His forever family, regardless of how messed up we are.

Tonight, before you tuck yourself in for the night, pray you will have the strength you need to accept people as they are, and to help us all be more understanding of those who are different from us, as they could be someone in your family.

# My "Adopted" Brother

## 1947–2004

Many of you met my "adopted" brother Tim Rogers. There were so many things I admired about him, it would take a complete book for me to pen the praises. The fondest memory I have is hearing his voice on the telephone, "Mikey, can I come over and play?" Humorous words from a quadraplegic veteran; words filled with joy.

Given the opportunity to describe Tim, these adjectives come to mind: loyal, honorable, passionate, dedicated, patriotic, and Christ-like. Now I know I've raised a few eyebrows with that last description, but those of you who met Timmy know what I mean. This was a man who was not always a believer . . . no way. In fact, he was 180 degrees out of phase with religion not all that many years ago. Let me tell you a little story about Tim and then you'll know why I wanted to include his story in this book on patriotism.

Like millions of young Americans in the Vietnam era, Tim was a rough and at times cocky guy who wanted to serve God, family, and country. As the war continued to escalate, Tim knew his draft notice was expected to arrive any day. To make sure he controlled his destiny, Tim decided to enlist in the United States Navy, with his goal being flight school. Tim's earliest memory was dreaming about becoming an aviator, and the dream was beginning to take wing.

His first duty assignment found Tim assigned to an SAR (Search Air Rescue) outfit where he was credited with saving many downed pilots who had ejected into the ocean, or had their aircraft shot out from under them in the jungles of Southeast Asia.

While awaiting orders to report to flight school, he was called to rescue a downed pilot floating somewhere in the vastness of the oceans off Vietnam. The turning point came that day as he rescued a downed Lt. Commander whose F-4 Phantom jet took a direct hit. As the story goes, this particular pilot was not doing too well in the choppy sea. He began to panic, threatening both himself and his rescuer. Tim, a 6'4" steely-eyed defender of American democracy, realized there was only one way to calm the frantic aviator — abolish all sensory conscious mental activity.

With a swift and powerful right hook, Tim transformed the stress-filled pilot into an unconscious subject with whom he could now work. Tim recalls thinking, *Oh, man, what have I done? I just punched the lights out of the Lt. Commander! I know my butt will be in deep trouble!*

Following the successful retrieval, the chopper landed aboard the aircraft carrier. Shortly after the chopper blades stopped turning, Tim got word he was wanted in the debriefing room. He knew he was in big trouble. But instead of being reprimanded, the Lt. Commander walked toward him holding out his right hand. The men vigorously shook hands, and while thanking Tim, he asked, "What is it you want to do in the navy, young man?"

"Become a pilot, sir." Tim replied.

"Well then, let's get you started on that mission."

But God had other plans for Tim Rogers. Before he could leave for basic flight school in Florida, one of the most incomprehensible accidents of war changed Tim's life forever. I won't go into the details of his injuries, but he sustained such damage the medics actually put a toe-tag on his body that read: "Watch this one, he comes and goes." Tim "went" 12 times and "came back" 12 times! And it was a miracle because God had more for him to accomplish on this earth.

*"Captain" Tim Rogers*

Thirty-five years later, Tim Rogers had become Branson's most-loved veteran. Tony Orlando called Tim his dearest friend. Being confined to a wheel-chair had its challenges, but Tim proved that physical impairments cannot hold back the spirit of God once its flame begins inside a patriot's heart. Tim was admired and respected for the man and patriot he became. He knew that God used him to heal the hearts and minds of the thousands of Vietnam veterans who came to Branson.

My heart glows with pride as I realize Tim was more than a man sitting in a wheelchair; he was truly a witness to his Lord's glory and the healing power of the Holy Spirit. When you come to Branson, stop by Mike Radford's Remember When Veterans Cafe inside the Radisson Hotel. It's dedicated to every veteran of all eras and I invite you to see the amazing tribute to service, along with Tim's photo, in uniform, and his dog tags.

# Letters to Home

Sometimes, I wonder if age is really a requirement for wisdom. There are so many opinions blowing across this great country of ours, as to whether the Americans belong in Iraq. Well, let me tell you . . . no, maybe Josh Peters should tell you. See, he's one of the "kids" who are fighting "over there," and, well, I think it's appropriate for us to step aside and let a genuine patriot explain what's in his heart. Maybe some of the president's critics can learn a thing or two.

### "A Sandy 4th of July"

I look at where I am — a country full of contempt for me, my uniform, and my flag. So far from home, yet memories so close to my heart. A desolate wilderness, which in comparison to the compassion of the enemy seems full of life.

*Spc. Josh Peters*

I look at what I am wearing. The uniform of a soldier. So proudly worn by my fathers before me. Life and death all summed up in a piece of clothing. The blood of my brethren stains my uniform. A sad reminder of the empty seat for Christmas that will never be filled.

I contemplate what I am thinking. How am I so fortunate? I am still alive, unhurt — save the memories of suffering Americans. I'll

never forget their faces. The expression as life leaves the body is burned into my memory. I pray their sacrifice isn't in vain. They are the heroes; I salute them on this hallowed day. I ponder what I'm feeling. Pride for my flag and dedication to my brothers in arms. Freedom cannot be explained, it may only be felt. Thanks to the ones before me, I will always have it. And I pray that what I have done will secure it for my children.

8/2/03

Family:

Hey, guys! Well, Happy Birthday to me. Not what I had in mind for celebration, but it's got to work, right? So how are things back home? Good I hope. Things are still slow here, thankfully. Time is dragging by, though. The word here now is March-April. Oh well, I guess I'll have to "cowboy up."

I decided to write a short story about my night in Al Ramadi. I figured it would paint a good picture of a night on the line. Hopefully it will give a face to the war that still rages "off camera." I'll be writing this "stream of consciousness" so just try to picture yourself there as my mind was sifting through a gauntlet of thoughts. I love and miss you all very much! — Josh

## One Night in Ramadi

As the sun sets I find a somewhat comfortable place in the back of my ambulance to try to get some much-needed sleep. The heat lies thick on my skin. I seem to be suspended in my own sweat. Every three seconds I swat at the mosquitoes and sand fleas that team up against my comfort. Their unsuccessful comrades that lie smashed and dead on my sticky skin doesn't seem to deter them at all. Off in the building behind me I hear fellow troopers playing poker. Their game too is interrupted by swatting, slapping, and swearing at the pests.

I try to ignore them by letting my mind drift. My eyes scan the inside of my ambulance. If these litters could talk! They have held the last wishes and words of patriotic heroes. This vehicle has seen death and dying along with the efforts of those trying to help the wounded cheat death. I can picture ghosts from previous missions lying there. Some screaming, some in disbelief, sorrow, and death itself. Their memory sometimes screams louder than the one that made it. It just seems to work that way.

As I try to put this out of my mind, I begin swatting again at the insects bent on destroying my flesh. Sweat stings my eyes and pools in my ears. The thoughts and heat are too much for me, so I move to the top of my vehicle. From there I can see our perimeter and every last star ever created. For now, it seems I have eluded the mosquitoes and fleas. But it is only a matter of time before their scouts find me and radio back to HQ about my new location.

I can't sleep. The roaming dogs barking and fighting keep me awake. It seems this whole country doesn't want me to sleep. I try something else. I think of my family. But them I decide not to ponder what they are doing for too long for fear of becoming homesick. I look at my watch, it reads 0200. Sure enough, the insects are back.

A mortar attack should be coming soon, I figured. The dogs, buzzing insects, the dogs, the sweating, the dogs, the swearing and slapping, the dogs . . . BOOM! A flash goes off near our perimeter. BOOM! Another one. I lock and load, waiting for a casualty to scream, "MEDIC!" I lay low on my vehicle, scanning the direction of the blast. The rattle of automatic gunfire sounds. The sweat stings my eyes. I no longer notice the bugs that have made a playground of my epidermis. RAT-TAT-TAT! I hear our 240s replying to the mortars. KA-BOOOOM! An Abrams tank clears her throat in the direction of the enemy. Silence. Nothing. I'm watching, listening waiting. Over the radio I hear "Trauma 6, Trauma 6. This is Lightning X-Ray, situation tight, out."

I make sure my weapon is back on "safe." I lay down, my heart slows. The dogs, the sweating, the swearing, the slapping. I slap until I get tired of slapping. I get up and make coffee. This country got the best of me tonight. No sleep, but I'm still alive. Thank God.

23 Sept. 03    1600    Iraq
Family —

Hello. Well, I have a lot to tell you. So I better get started. We got a call the other night around 2100 that a TCP (Traffic Control Point) team got hit with an IED [Improvised Explosive Device]. Within minutes my ambulance was linking up with our security at the front gate. Off we went into the not-so-friendly town of Ramadi.

It is pitch black and the prime hour for an attack. All senses are on overload. After crossing the Euphrates to the east side of Ramadi, we come to the spot where they were hit. As soon as we pull up, the enemy opens up with small arms fire. Ambush. With one fluid motion, I put the brake on, grabbed my aid bag and M-16, and half rolled, half flipped out of my vehicle and dropped my silhouette behind the front left tire. I have seen the effects of AK rounds on Humvees, and I didn't want to be there.

The familiar sounds of "whiz, zing, ping, and thwack" filled the air around me. "Contact, contact, 3 o'clock," someone yelled. "Is anyone hit?" I yelled. No response was a good response. I dared a look to the direction of the enemy, pitch black except for muzzle flashes. They were everywhere and nowhere.

I roll to the front of my vehicle, move my selector switch from safety to 3-round burst and await the command. I aim for the closest muzzle flash. "Don't fire!" "We have an LRS [Long Range Surveillance] team out there somewhere!" "Whoosh!" We send a flare up, hoping to see them hidden in the overgrowth of the river. Nothing, no more gunfire.

I learn the IED victim was KIA. With a wife at home, eight months pregnant. I roll back behind the tire, praying they don't have RPGs [Rocket Propelled Grenade]. If they do, we are dead. "Is anyone hit?" I yell again. No, everyone's good so far. Two fire teams are sent out to patrol where the firing was coming from. For two hours we were there, taking fire, NVGs [Night Vision Goggles] on, no luck even seeing them. People were even driving boats up the river so they could shoot at us. We captured seven that night, and 3/3 lost its first soldier.

It was the longest night of my life. I cannot describe to you the feeling of getting shot at while dismounted at night without being able to see the enemy or fire back because of friendlies in the area. I don't think I have ever prayed so hard in my life. I have been shot at before, but never at night, in the middle of town. I can still shut my eyes and see it all. It's weird how some things stay with you. The poor guy that died had his blood and brain matter sprayed on the driver, so cleaning him up wasn't exactly easy either.

Ever since the 82nd and SF [Special Forces] started stirring things up, there has been something every night. I don't think it will get better anytime soon. I'm doing fine, though. Saying my prayers, brushing my teeth, and all that. We finally got the word on coming home. Out of Iraq

by early Feb, load vehicles early March, last soldier home by 15 April. Keep me in your prayers as you are in mine. I love and miss you all very much. Please don't worry about me. Dad, you'd be proud, I used all my hunting skills that night. Looking for odd shapes, dogs and bird sounds. It kept me from making any wrong moves. Keep the mail coming!

Your son & brother, Josh

### "Thoughts of Home"

When we are faced with challenges, as we often are in life, one is apt to become pensive, and yet, confused. During this time of trial I have found myself growing more and more thankful for the blessing of a loving home.

I remember how my father looked at me after we won a baseball game — with pride. I remember how he looked at me after we lost — with pride. In fact, as I recall all of the hobbies and interests my father and I have undertaken over my past 23 years, I recall nothing but patience, joy, and pride. I tried my best to please my father, not for fear of his wrath, but for fear of his disappointment in me. The latter wrenching my heart much more than the former. My father and I have crossed Europe together, spent stormy nights in tents together and, as odd as this is to say, grown older together. I've found I will never outgrow his advice. The traits that my sweetheart loves me for now are traits that I have gathered from my father. He has chosen a life of service, second only to his family. Perhaps that is why my life feels incomplete unless I am serving. He demonstrated love and respect for my mother for my brother and me to follow. I hope I may one day be half the man he is.

Behind every selfless action my father displayed for us boys was my mother, a strong woman whose lap I will never outgrow. As I was growing up, she was the moral beacon through what would have otherwise been "the shipwreck of puberty." Always there in the stands, wearing her sons' faces on buttons with pride, yelling her encouragement for us (and her displeasure of the call at times). Always on her boys' side when it came time to talk my father into putting up the outdoor Christmas lights (which he always did, never failing to include the frustration of the process in a sermon!) Her voice and love always speak of a woman who will be on my side. She was the perfect referee for two little boys' scuffles and the pillar of support for our father. I pray that I will marry a woman as strong as she one day. These days my visits home are rare, but she never fails to have one of my favorite meals — chicken enchiladas — ready for me. Sacrificing her own time and desires to put me through college, I thank her for providing me with a priceless education. Her closet reveals countless clothing items that represent organizations of which her children have been a part: baseball teams, basketball teams, colleges, even the army, and her yellow ribbon for me now. The dedication to God and family is unparalleled in her life. My brother and I always get priority.

My brother is now full steam ahead on his way to adulthood also. I don't seem to remember that transition. Unfortunately, it seemed to pass me by as I was engulfed in my own college graduation and then soon after departed to spend some time with Uncle Sam. Despite the story of feeding him poison berries, I'm glad he is around. His dedication to book study is an inspiration to me. We are so alike in attributes and activities, yet have incredible differences, too. Now in this faraway place, I wish I could go back to our Little League days together. Perhaps because that was the last time I was taller than him . . . and better looking. I remember our walks through stores. The girls always talked to him and I was the one trying to look cool! I guess life isn't always fair. From our

late night hockey tournaments on PlayStation to early morning hunting expeditions, I cherish every memory. Now on his way to being grown, I only hope he knows I will always be "available," even when I can't physically be there. The bond of brotherhood is beyond love. It is an unspoken truce and treaty, protection of each other to the end.

As I said, I'm lucky. I have no idea what fighting parents are like. No clue whatsoever what drugs and excessive alcohol can do to a family. I've seen examples, but never experienced it. I try to make my parents and brother proud of me. I feel they are even when they don't agree with my decisions. Do they want their son at war? No. Are they bursting with pride when a stranger asks about me? Most certainly.

As I look to complete this chapter of my life, I look to the next with hopes of continuing the tradition of love and respect I have grown up knowing. One day I hope to be as good a coach as my father, marry someone as loving and supportive as my mother, and have friendships that will last as long as my bond with my brother. Dad, Mom, Justin: Thank you so much for providing me with the strength I need to perform the awesome task at hand. You all at home are the heroes; I love you all.

Josh

Saturday, 13 Sep 03    1136    Iraq


Note: Josh returned safely to his beloved homeland and is now stationed at Fort Collins, Colorado.

# SECTION TWO

## Teachers

## *Impact for Life*

When I was still little "Mikey," there were two teachers who stand out in my memory. One was a cheerful but rather large woman, Mrs. Sparks; the other came along many years later, his name was Dr. Weatherspoon. Let me tell you a little about Mrs. Sparks.

As with every first day of school, my third grade was particularly stressful. It was a mixture of excitement and hopeful anticipation. "Oh, please God, make her nice, make her like me!" I'd pray. The third grade was going to be a major turning point in my life. It would be the last time I would attend Olive View School in Corning, California; the final months playing with my buddy Earl Benning, who would soon move to Edinburgh, Scotland; and unknown to me, we, too, would pack our things into a moving van and head down Highway 99 to live in Sacramento.

But in the last few months under the tutelage of Mrs. Sparks, two major lessons were about to be learned. We were making Christmas ornaments that day — remember those red and green strips of construction paper cut into thin pieces, then slapped together with white paste? It was my assignment to use the paper cutter, and with precision and great care I returned to my work area with a stack of soon-to-be rings to add to the paper chain destined to adorn our class Christmas tree.

"Mikey!" I heard Mrs. Sparks say, "Come over here right now." Her usual soft and gentle approach to education had suddenly taken on a serious tone. I shuffled past my little buddies and looked up at my teacher who was obviously not pleased with something I had done.

"Yes, Mrs. Sparks," I said sheepishly. I stood next to her with the top of my head barely reaching her waistline. She pointed to the paper cutter sitting atop the work-table.

"What's this?" She asked.

"A paper cutter." I shyly replied.

Gazing down at me she tilted her head to one side and said, "And just what might happen if someone were to put their little fingers under that blade that you've left up?"

I got the point. Isn't it funny how something as trivial as this paper cutter sticks so vividly in my mind. To this day I never leave a paper cutter with the blade not securely fastened. My wife, Shari, thinks it's funny how I'm obsessed with paper cutters being closed. But you know what? I guess the lesson here is that our teachers really do have a huge impact on shaping our lives. Thank you, Mrs. Sparks, not only for the paper cutter lesson but all the kindness you gave to your students.

Years later another teacher would impact my life and create the passion I have for American history and patriotism. His name was Dr. Weatherspoon. In 1965, I had the honor of attending his class during my first semester at American River College. Dr. Weatherspoon was blind, or should I say "sightless," because this man "saw" so much history and reached his students in such dynamic ways. We all had teachers who seemed to go through the motions, but lacked any passion in what they did. Professor Weatherspoon was different. This man was enthusiastic . . . electric! This was an educator.

The morning sunlight streamed into the lecture hall as we prepared for the first of many gripping lectures by a professor who was widely known as one of the college's best. We were studying the American Revolution. Professor Weatherspoon quietly entered the large room, his German Shepherd guide dog leading the way across the stage. The elegant and graceful canine carefully guided his master to the podium. The class sat in silence, awaiting our first day's instructions. The professor stood erect, hands resting on each side of the lectern. We continued to sit in polite silence, seconds ticking away until each of us became a little uncomfortable. Minutes passed, some students began to squirm in their seats as the professor stood silent, staring out into the darkness straight ahead of him. Then with the swiftness of a lightening bolt he shouted, "General Cornwallis and the red coats began to charge the unprepared minutemen! Gunpowder flashed as muskets spewed their deadly balls of lead — projectiles zipped through the air hitting their targets . . . ripping flesh and shattering bones of the enemy!" From the moment Dr. Weatherspoon began to speak, every student was "there," inside the story he was painting in our imagination. His style and flair for the dramatic would forever influence me. It was this teacher more than any other who shaped my love for history.

What is the lesson here? Be enthusiastic. Show your passion about something, then others will listen to what you have to say.

# "All Good Things"

*by Sister Helen P. Mrosia*

**(Authors note: tissues will be needed for this story.)**

He was in the very first third grade class I taught at Saint Mary's School in Morris, Minnesota. All 34 of my students were dear to me, but Mark Eklund was one in a million. He was very neat, but had that happy-to-be-alive attitude that made even his occasional mischievousness delightful.

Mark talked incessantly. I had to remind him again and again that talking without permission was not acceptable. What impressed me so much though, was his sincere response every time I had to correct him for misbehaving — "Thank you for correcting me, Sister!" I didn't know what to make of it at first, but before long I became accustomed to hearing it many times a day.

One morning my patience was growing thin when Mark talked once too often, and then I made a novice-teacher's mistake. I looked at him and said, "If you say one more word, I'm going to tape your mouth shut!"

It wasn't ten seconds later when another student blurted out, "Mark is talking again!" I had to act. I remember the scene as if it occurred this morning. I walked to my desk, very deliberately opened my drawer and took out a roll of masking tape and without saying a word proceeded

to Mark's desk, tore off two pieces, and made a big X over his mouth. I then returned to the front of the room. As I glanced back at Mark to see how he was doing, he winked at me! That did it. I started laughing as the whole class cheered as I walked back to Mark and removed the tape. I shrugged my shoulders and his first words were, "Thank you for correcting me, Sister!"

At the end of the year I was asked to teach junior high math. The years flew by, and before I knew it Mark was in my classroom again. He was more handsome than ever and just as polite. Since he had to listen carefully to my instructions in the "new math" he did not talk as much in the ninth grade as he had in the third.

One Friday, things just didn't feel right in the classroom. The students were all depressed and I sensed their frustration. I had to stop this crankiness before it got out of hand, so I asked them to list the names of the other students in the room and list all the things they liked about each other. It took the remainder of the class period to finish the assignment, and as the students left the room, each handed me the papers. Mark said, "Thank you for teaching me, Sister. Have a good weekend."

That Saturday, I wrote down the name of each student on a separate sheet of paper and listed what everyone else had said about that individual. On Monday I gave each student his or her list. Before long, the entire class was smiling. "Really?" I heard whispered. "I never knew that meant anything to anyone." Another said, "I didn't know others like me so much!"

No one ever mentioned those papers in class again. I never knew if they discussed them after class or with their parents, but it didn't matter. The exercise had accomplished its purpose. The students were happy with themselves and one another again.

That group of students moved on. Several years later, after I returned from a vacation, my parents met me at the airport. As we were driving home, Mother asked me the usual questions about the trip, the weather, my experiences in general.

There was a light lull in the conversation when Mother gave Dad a sideways glance and simply said, "Dad?" My father cleared his throat as he usually did before something important.

"The Eklunds called last night," he began.

"Really?" I said. "I haven't heard from them in years. I wonder how Mark is doing."

Dad responded quietly. "Mark was killed in Vietnam last week," he said. "The funeral is tomorrow and his parents would like it if you could attend." To this day, I can still point to the exact spot on I-494 where my dad told me about Mark.

I had never seen a serviceman in a military coffin before. Dear Mark looked so handsome, so mature. All I could think at that moment was, *Mark, I would give all the masking tape in the world if only you would talk to me!*

The church was packed with Mark's friends. Why did it have to rain on the day of the funeral? It was difficult enough at the graveside. The pastor said the usual prayers, and the bugler played "Taps." One by one, those who loved Mark took a last walk by the coffin and sprinkled it with holy water. I was the last one to bless the coffin. As I stood there, one of the soldiers who had acted as pallbearer came up to me and asked, "Were you Mark's math teacher?" I nodded as I continued to stare at the coffin. "Mark talked about you all the time," he said.

After the funeral, most of Mark's former classmates headed to Chuck's farmhouse for lunch. Mark's mother and father were there, obviously

waiting for me. "We want you to know something," his father said, taking a wallet out of his pocket. "They found this on Mark when he was killed. We thought you might recognize it." Opening the billfold, he carefully removed two worn pieces of notebook paper that had obviously been taped, folded, and refolded many times. I knew without looking that the papers were the ones on which I had listed all the good things each of Mark's classmates had said about him.

"Thank you so much for doing that," Mark's mother said. "As you can see, Mark treasured it."

Mark's classmates started to gather around us. Charlie smiled rather sheepishly and said, "I still have my list. It's in the top drawer of my desk."

Chuck's wife said, "Chuck asked me to put this in our wedding album."

I have mine, too," Marilyn said. "It's in my diary."

Then Vicki, another classmate reached into her pocketbook, took out her wallet and showed her worn and frazzled list to the group. "I carry this with me at all times," Vicki said without batting an eyelash. "I think we all saved our lists."

That's when I finally sat down and began to cry. I cried for Mark and for all his friends who would never see him again.

(Originally sent by Dorothy Watson, Columbia, Missouri).[2]

# The Little Things

*Author unknown*

I had a very special teacher in high school many years ago whose husband unexpectedly died of a heart attack. About a week after his death, she shared some of her insight with a classroom of students. As the late afternoon sunlight came streaming in through the classroom windows, and the class was nearly over, she moved a few things aside on the edge of her desk and sat down. With a gentle look of reflection on her face, she paused and said, "Before class is over, I would like to share with all of you a thought that is unrelated to class, but which I feel is very important.

"Each of us is put here on earth to learn, share, love, appreciate, and give of ourselves. None of us knows when this fantastic experience will end. It can be taken away at any moment. Perhaps this is God's way of telling us that we must make the most out of every single day." Her eyes were beginning to water, but she went on, "So I would like you all to make me a promise. From now on, en route to school, or on your way home, you will find something beautiful to notice. It doesn't have to be something you see. It could be a scent of freshly baked bread wafting from an open window. It could be the sound of the breeze slightly rustling the leaves in the trees, or the way the morning light catches one autumn leaf as it falls gently to the ground. Please, look for these things

and cherish them. For although it may sound trite to some, these things are the 'essence' of life. The little things we are put here on earth to enjoy. The things we often take for granted. We must make it important to notice them, for at any time it can all be taken away."

The class was completely quiet. We all picked up our books and filed out of the room silently. That afternoon, I noticed more things on my way home from school than I had that whole semester. Every once in a while, I think of that teacher and remember what an impression she made on all of us, and I try to appreciate all of those things that sometimes we all overlook. Take notice of something special on your lunch hour or commute home today. Go barefoot. Or walk by the water at sunset. Stop on the way home and enjoy a double dip ice cream cone before dinner! For as we get older, it is not the things we did that we often regret, but the things we didn't do.

# Her Name Was Mrs. Thompson

*(Author unknown — have tissues ready again.)*

A s she stood in front of her fifth grade class on the very first day of school, she told the children a lie: no one would be favored. Like most teachers, she looked at some students as impossible. There in the front row, slumped in his seat, was a little boy named Teddy Stoddard.

Mrs. Thompson had watched Teddy the year before and noticed that he didn't play well with the other children, that his clothes were messy, and that he constantly needed a bath. And Teddy could be unpleasant. It got to the point where Mrs. Thompson would actually take delight in marking his papers with a broad red pen, making bold X's and then putting a big "F" at the top of his papers.

At the school where Mrs. Thompson taught, she was required to review each child's past records and she put Teddy's off until last. However, when she reviewed his file, she was in for a surprise.

Teddy's first grade teacher wrote, "Teddy is a bright child with a ready laugh. He does his work neatly and has good manners . . . he is a joy to be around."

His second grade teacher wrote, "Teddy is an excellent student, well liked by his classmates, but he is troubled because his mother has a terminal illness and life at home must be a struggle."

★ ★ ★ 55 ★ ★ ★

His third grade teacher wrote, "His mother's death has been hard on him. He tries to do his best, but his father doesn't show much interest and his home life will soon affect him if some steps aren't taken." Teddy's fourth grade teacher wrote, "Teddy is withdrawn and doesn't show much interest in school. He doesn't have many friends and he sometimes sleeps in class."

By now, Mrs. Thompson realized the problem, and she was ashamed of herself. She felt even worse when her students brought her Christmas presents, wrapped in beautiful ribbons and bright paper, except for Teddy's. His present was clumsily wrapped in the heavy, brown paper that he got from a grocery bag. Mrs. Thompson took pains to open it in the middle of the other presents.

Some of the children started to laugh when she found a rhinestone bracelet with some of the stones missing and a bottle that was one quarter full of perfume. But she stifled the children's laughter when she exclaimed how pretty the bracelet was putting it on and dabbing some of the perfume on her wrist. Teddy Stoddard stayed after school that day just long enough to say, "Mrs. Thompson, today you smelled just like my mom used to." After the children left, she cried for at least an hour. On that very day, she quit teaching reading and writing and arithmetic. Instead, she began to teach children.

Mrs. Thompson paid particular attention to Teddy. As she worked with him, his mind seemed to come alive. The more she encouraged him, the faster he responded. By the end of the year, Teddy had become one of the smartest children in the class and, despite her lie that she would love all the children the same, Teddy became one of her "teacher's pets." A year later, she found a note under her door from Teddy, telling her that she was still the best teacher he had in his life.

Six years went by before she got another note from Teddy. He then wrote that he had finished high school, third in his class, and she was still the best teacher he ever had in his whole life. Four years after that, she got another letter saying that while things had been tough at times, he'd stayed in school, had stuck with it, and would soon graduate from college with the highest of honors. He assured Mrs. Thompson that she was still the best and favorite teacher he ever had in his whole life.

Then four more years passed and yet another letter came. This time he explained that after he got his bachelor's degree, he decided to go a little further. The letter explained that she was still the best and favorite teacher he ever had. But now his name was a little longer — the letter was signed "Theodore F. Stoddard, M.D."

The story doesn't end there. Soon, there was another letter that spring. Teddy said he'd met this girl and was going to be married. He explained that his father had died a couple of years ago, and he was wondering if Mrs. Thompson might agree to sit in the place at the wedding that was usually reserved for the mother of the groom. Of course, Mrs. Thompson did. And guess what? She wore that bracelet, the one with several rhinestones missing. And she made sure she was wearing the perfume that Teddy remembered his mother wearing on their last Christmas together. They hugged each other, and Dr. Stoddard whispered in Mrs. Thompson's ear, "Thank you, Mrs. Thompson, for believing in me. Thank you so much for making me feel important and showing me that I could make a difference."

Mrs. Thompson, with tears in her eyes, whispered back. She said, "Teddy, you have it all wrong. You were the one who taught me that I could make a difference. I didn't know how to teach until I met you."

Warm someone's heart today . . . pass this story along to someone you care about. Remember, wherever you go and whatever you do, you will have the opportunity to touch someone's heart and change their view of themselves and the world. Be a mentor.

Teachers are the most important influences on our nation's young minds. They have enormous power to motivate us to greatness or destroy the dreamer. Lucky for me, I had some pretty great people who shared my passions for God, family, and country. In my opinion, teachers are some of the greatest heroes in our society. They are the frontline role models for our nation's children.

# SECTION THREE

*Patriots*

# What Is a Veteran? What Is a Patriot?

Shari and I were blessed to work in the entertainment industry and have our own theater in Branson. Every day we'd pinch ourselves to see if it were real because we were having so much fun performing and making people laugh, cry, and remember the fun things in their lives. "The Remember When Show," known as a nostalgic patriotic comedy, continued to grow year after year, and we know why. We believe God is using us to do His work, and one of the hardest things to do is "get out of His way and let Him control whatever it is that He wants us to do!" Does that make sense? Anyway, when I began to consider what to write in regard to veterans and patriots, it became clear to me. Tell true stories of those men and women who epitomize the subject, people we know personally.

When we define the word "veteran," Webster's says, "a person who served in the armed forces, an old experienced soldier." I have to laugh when I think about actually putting into print what my mind just flashed upon because some may not understand my sense of humor. If you've been to my show or heard my speeches, this is what caused me to chuckle when I first read the definition of a veteran. My first "vision" of a veteran as described (an old experienced soldier) was of a man whom

I have grown to love, even though I respected him tremendously long before we met. The name of this "old experienced soldier" is Judge Robert Decatur, one of the famed "Tuskegee Airmen" from WWII. Trish Thompson, one of Branson's leading veteran advocates first introduced us, and for that Shari and I are forever grateful. Trish, a vivacious blonde, affectionately called "Trish the dish" by the famed flyers, is one of two women designated as an honorary "Tuskegee Airman." The other — Ms. Lena Horne!

Now I must confess Bob Decatur is not that old. True, he's in his eighties, but he looks and carries himself with the stride of a man far younger. Getting to know Robert Decatur is one of our life's highest personal rewards. He's truly a patriot in every sense of the word. Bob grew up in Cleveland, Ohio, and even played professional baseball in the old Negro National League. His teammates were the likes of Jackie Robinson,

*Mike, with Judge Robert Decatur, "Tuskegee Airman"*

Satchel Paige, and Buck O'Neil. This is a man who always excelled in everything he did, and epitomizes the term "excellence."

As a young man who finished college at 20, he soon embarked on his military duty. And, of course, his military aspiration was to become a fighter pilot. Only one problem with that lofty goal — there were no black aviators, period. You must remember, during WWII this was literally out of the question because "Negroes" were considered intellectually incapable of flying an airplane. But our friend Bob Decatur is a man who dreams big dreams, then makes them happen. Any obstacles in his way are just challenges to be defeated.

As a young black airman cadet, he dreamed of flying P-51 Mustangs. He wanted to fight for his country and to defend his nation, a nation for which he would have given his life. What amazes me about Bob's patriotism is his dedication to God, family, and country, even though he lived in a nation where most blacks weren't allowed to vote, drink water from the same public drinking fountains, or eat at the same restaurants. Thank God, times changed. Recently, at one of the national conventions for the "Tuskegee Airmen," General Colin Powell addressed the distinguished audience and said, "You are my heroes . . . it is upon your backs I rose to achieve my success. You are the wind beneath my wings!"

Bob Decatur's life is a rare testimony to the triumph of the human spirit to succeed beyond all odds and Bob became the mentor for the likes of Colin Powell. Oh, there is one other achiever Bob inspired and called his friend — Dr. Martin Luther King Jr. Bob remembers being with Dr. King the night before the assassination. He remembers saying, "Now Dr. King, don't you go down to Memphis and get yourself killed." It was the last thing they laughed about together.

Today, we look at the career of this amazing man and marvel at his accomplishments. If you have seen the movie "The Tuskegee Airmen" you might recall the scene where all the cadets had to retake an exam because one cadet scored a perfect 100 percent on a very difficult test. It was Bob Decatur. Another scene in the movie shows an airman developing engine problems and forced to land on a country road. Again, it was Bob Decatur.

Shari and I marvel at the fact we now call him our friend. Bob Decatur — former WWII aviator, attorney, honored judge, proud family man, and father. Robert Decatur's life has been a blessing to his country, and a testimony to the triumph of a young man's dreams. His experiences are the "stuff" of legends. How many of us can say our friends were Jackie Robinson, Dr. Martin Luther King, Satchel Paige, and Buck O'Neil? How many of us can say we became a federal judge, an ambassador of the United States, and a famed military aviator? We consider ourselves lucky to call him our friend.

In 1998, we had another amazing man sitting in our audience in Branson. His name is Col. Ben Purcell, and although I had no idea who he was, or what he did, this gentle man was to become one of our dearest friends, a man who is respected and loved by all who have the honor of knowing him. Ben has the distinction of being the highest-ranking army officer held as a POW in the Vietnam war. He and his lovely wife, Anne, were passing through Branson on their way to the 25th anniversary of his unit's release. In every sense of the word, these men are true patriots and real American heroes. It is unfathomable to understand their experiences or the evil each POW suffered at the hands of the Communists who seemed to "enjoy" the pain they inflicted on our men. Col. Purcell was held in solitary confinement inside the famous "Hanoi Hilton."

*With Army Colonel Ben Purcell,*
*who spent 5-1/2 years in the "Hanoi Hilton"*

Today, his love of the Lord shines through his eyes and crosses his face in every easy smile he flashes. It was his faith in the Almighty that got him through it all. And he told us that many of his prison mates died because they had no faith to carry them through. I asked him what he felt was the greatest blessing living as a free man. He looked toward the clear blue sky and in his easy Georgian style said, "The ability to rise in the morning and go for a walk. The liberty to stop and smell a flower, or the freedom to simply gaze into the blue skies of America and take in the deep sense of wonder. To feel the amazing joy that fills your heart knowing you are free!" He escaped several times but was then recaptured again and again, until finally being released when the war came to a close.

The last time they came to Branson, I asked Col. Purcell and his wife, Anne, to stand so I could introduce them to my audience. The crowd jumped to their feet and gave them a long, rousing, standing ovation. His eyes filled with tears as the entire theater stood in honor of this true patriot. Col. Purcell came up on the stage and shyly waved his "thanks" as is his style. The Purcells are not much on self-promotion. He slowly walked across the stage with that smile flashing across his face. I joined him in a bear hug. Hugging was something he liked to do because affection was a luxury he hadn't experienced in the long years spent in a Communist prison.

His eyes moist, he turned toward the crowd which now sat silently. "In 5½ years in solitary confinement, I laughed only two times . . . and today seeing "The Remember When Show" and being with all of you . . . my cup runneth over." The sold-out crowd jumped to their feet again, cheering and applauding one of America's true patriots.

When you came to our theater, just outside the entrance you'd see our first Hall of Heroes. There are hundreds of photographs and military memorabilia from every corner of our nation and Canada. Our Hall inside the Radisson is nearly 1,000 feet in length. One extraordinary display at the Radisson includes Col. Purcell's uniform, covered with medals and commendations. It is the

*Mike presents Ross Perot with the "Ambassador Award" for all his POW/MIA work.*

very uniform he wore "home" when our men were finally released from the hell they experienced in North Vietnam. Looking at Ben's uniform and the pictures taken only days before his release from captivity will touch you deeply. I hope you can come to Branson for the experience. We have created a Veterans Cafe, R & R Bar, and Canteen to honor our servicemen and women. Be sure to stop by and take a look at all the memorabilia. It will make you proud.

*Three dates that were turning points in American history:*

July 4, 1776
December 7, 1941
September 11, 2001

We will always remember. . . .

# The Veterans

Author unknown

They are the ones who endure constant pain from a bullet fired 50 years ago . . . or smile back at the innocent child who stares at his missing limb. She's the gal who raises her children to obey God's laws . . . then answers the call as her outfit is called to Desert Storm and finds herself sweltering in the Saudi desert . . . while 10,000 miles away her kids cry themselves to sleep while asking their daddy, "When's Mommy coming home?" He's the POW who still screams in the night — and dreams of the day his MIA buddies will all come home. She's the lady who checks out your groceries and always has a smile for you even though her head aches from an unknown sickness she picked up in Somalia. She's the woman who tucks in her children at night, saying bedtime prayers with them as she silently prays for the children who were made orphans by blazing bullets in Bosnia, Belfast, Boston. . . .

He's the cop in your neighborhood who limps from the shrapnel in his leg, or the bartender who pours you beer and remembers his buddies who were with him in Nam and a second later vaporized from a VC mortar. . . . She's the nurse in Saigon who worked 20-hour days hoping against hope she could save every kid who came in, then sobbed herself to sleep every night when she couldn't. He's a veteran named Jimmie Reese who, while with the Yankees in '31 called Babe Ruth his "roomie," and at the age of 92 smiled and said, "Never regret growing old . . . for many are denied the privilege."

These and thousands more just like them are the true patriots — the heroes of our society. It's up to you and me to ensure their sacrifices and legacy live forever. Our nation's destiny demands nothing less.

*Veterans on stage during the "Remember When Show"*

*Veterans are always honored during every show or speech.*

# a Dad's Message to Congress

On Thursday, May 27, 1999, Darrell Scott, the father of Rachel Scott, a victim of the Columbine High School shootings in Littleton, Colorado, was invited to address the House Judiciary Committee's sub-committee. What he said to our national leaders during this special session of Congress was painfully truthful. They were not prepared for what he was to say, nor was it received well. It needs to be heard by every parent, politician, sociologist, psychologist, and so-called expert. These courageous words spoken by Darrell Scott are powerful, penetrating, and deeply personal. There is no doubt that God sent this man as a voice crying in the wilderness. The following is a portion of the transcript of his comments:

Since the dawn of creation there has been both good and evil in the hearts of men and women. We all contain the seeds of kindness or the seeds of violence. The death of my wonderful daughter, Rachel Joy Scott, and the death of that heroic teacher, and the other 11 children who died must not be in vain. Their blood cries out for answers.

The first recorded act of violence was when Cain slew his brother Abel out in the field. The villain was not the club he used. Neither was it the NCA, the National Club Association.

The true killer was Cain, and the reason for the murder could only be found in Cain's heart.

In the days that followed the Columbine tragedy, I was amazed at how quickly fingers began to be pointed at groups such as the NRA. I am not a member of the NRA. I am not a hunter. I do not even own a gun. I am not here to represent or defend the NRA because I don't believe that they are responsible for my daughter's death. Therefore I do not believe that they need to be defended. If I believed they had anything to do with Rachel's murder I would be their strongest opponent.

I am here today to declare that Columbine was not just a tragedy — it was a spiritual event that should be forcing us to look at where the real blame lies! Much of the blame lies here in this room. Much of the blame lies behind the pointing fingers of the accusers themselves. I wrote a poem just four nights ago that expresses my feelings best. This was written way before I knew I would be speaking here today:

> Your laws ignore our deepest needs,
> your words are empty air.
> You've stripped away our heritage,
> you've outlawed simple prayer.
> Now gunshots fill our classrooms,
> and precious children die.
> You seek for answers everywhere,
> and ask the question; "Why?"
> You regulate restrictive laws,
> through legislative creed.

And yet you fail to understand,
that God is what we need!

Men and women are three-part beings. We all consist of
body, soul, and spirit. When we refuse to acknowledge a third
part of our make-up, we create a void that allows evil, prejudice,
and hatred to rush in and wreak havoc. Spiritual influences were
present within our educational systems for most of our nation's
history. Many of our major colleges began as theological semi-
naries. This is a historical fact.

What has happened to us as a nation? We have refused to
honor God, and in so doing, we open the doors to hatred and
violence. And when something as terrible as Columbine's tragedy occurs — politicians immediately look for a scapegoat such
as the NRA. They immediately seek to pass more restrictive laws
that . . . erode away our personal and private liberties. We do
not need more restrictive laws. Eric and Dylan would not have
been stopped by metal detectors. No amount of gun laws can
stop someone who spends months planning this type of mas-
sacre.

The real villain lies within our own political posturing, and
restrictive legislation is not the answer. The young people of our
nation hold the key. There is a spiritual awakening taking place
that will not be squelched! We do not need more religion. We
do not need more gaudy television evangelists spewing out verbal
religious garbage. We do not need more million-dollar church
buildings built while people with basic needs are being ignored.
We do need a change of heart and a humble acknowledgment

that this nation was founded on the principle of simple trust in God!

As my son Craig lay under that table in the school library and saw his two friends murdered before his very eyes — he did not hesitate to pray in school. I defy any law or politician to deny him that right! I challenge every young person in America, and around the world, to realize that on April 20, 1999, at Columbine High School, prayer was brought back to our schools. Do not let the many prayers offered by those students be in vain. Dare to move into the new millennium with a sacred disregard for legislation that violates your God-given right to communicate with Him.

To those of you who would point your finger at the NRA I give to you a sincere challenge. Dare to examine your own heart before casting the first stone! My daughter's death will not be in vain! The young people of this country will not allow that to happen![3]

Ask yourself this question: "What am I feeling right now?" When I first read this, my heart ached for the parents of these innocent kids. They were so young, filled with the expectations of fulfilling their "American Dream." There are no words that will erase the heartbreak; there are no medications to heal the wounds in their hearts — only lessons. But will people really learn? Did you really hear this father's words? The message I take from the Columbine tragedy is the same one to be learned in New York City — our nation is truly at great risk, not only from terrorists from the Middle East, but of our own as well. When kids don't learn "Thou Shalt Not Kill" it leaves them open to the evil that sometimes creeps in and takes over their hearts.

# *Granny D's Day in Court*

Most of us saw Doris "Granny D" Haddock as she marched across America in 1999. She was hiking to draw attention to her passionate belief in campaign finance reform. I sat and marveled at her energy and her spunk; and it was obvious she was a patriot of the first order, a favorite of the nightly news. This was a great story — aging woman marching across our land to send a message to young and old alike. But what shocks me is the manner in which she was treated once she arrived in Washington, D.C. You will be shaking your head when you learn what happened, because she violated no law.

On Wednesday, May 24, 1999, in the District of Columbia court, Granny D pled guilty to the charge of demonstrating in the Capitol building on April 21. Some 31 others were charged with her. This is a story I know you will pass along to all your friends who care about this land and who fear for the rights of even the weakest of our society. Try not to get as angry as I did; it's not good for your blood pressure.

Doris and the demonstrators were represented in court by attorney Mark Goldstone, who provided his services at a reduced rate. Doris and friends then picketed the $26 million dollar Democratic Party fundraiser at the Washington MCI Arena, where $500,000 fat cats sat at tables on the arena floor eating barbecue while listening to the president and vice president. The "regular people," the $50 contributors, had to pay $3 for a bottle of water to watch the others eat. Doris was well interviewed there by National Public Radio and several newspapers. When she crossed the street in front of the security-bristling arena, she was approached by a squad of six D.C. police. Soon thereafter she was arrested.

The May 24, 2000, court statement of Doris Haddock:

> Your Honor, the old woman who stands before you was arrested for reading the Declaration of Independence in America's Capitol Building. I did not raise my voice to do so and I blocked no hall. The First Amendment to the Constitution, Your Honor, says that Congress shall make no law abridging the freedom of speech, or of the press; or the right of the people peaceably to assemble and to petition the government for a redress of grievances. So I cannot imagine what legitimate law I could have broken. We peaceably assembled there, Your Honor, careful to not offend the rights of any other citizen nor interrupt the peaceful enjoyment of their day. The people we met were supportive of what we were saying and I think they — especially the children — were shocked that we would be arrested for such a thoroughly wholesome American activity as respectfully voicing our opinion in our own hall. Any American standing there would have been shocked.

> For we were a most peaceable assembly, until the police came in with their bullhorns and their shackles to arrest us. One of us, who is here today, was injured and required a number of stitches to his head after he fell and could not break his own fall. He was detained for over four hours without medical care. I am glad we were only reading from the Declaration of Independence. I shudder to think what might have happened had we read from the Bill of Rights. I was reading from the Declaration of Independence to

make the point that we must declare our independence from the corrupting bonds of big money in our election campaigns.

And so I was reading these very words when my hands were pulled behind me and bound: "We hold these truths to be self-evident, that all men are created equal, that they are endowed by their Creator with certain unalienable rights, that among these are life, liberty and the pursuit of happiness. That to secure these rights, governments are instituted among men, deriving their just powers from the consent of the governed — that whenever any form of government becomes destructive of these ends, it is the right of the people to alter or to abolish it."

Your Honor, we would never seek to abolish our dear United States. But alter it? Yes. It is our constant intention that it should be a government of, by, and for the people, not the special interests, so that people may use this government in service to each other's needs and to protect the condition of our earth. Your Honor, it is now your turn to be a part of this arrest. If your concern is that we might have interfered with the visitor's right to a meaningful tour of their Capitol, I tell you that we helped them have a more meaningful one. If your concern is that we might have been blocking the halls of our government, let me assure you that we stood to one side of the rotunda where we would not be in anyone's way. But I inform you that the halls are indeed blocked over there. They are blocked by the shameless sale of public policy to campaign contributors, which bars the doors and the halls to the people's legitimate needs and the flow of proper representation.

We Americans must put an end to it in any peaceful way that we can. Yes, we can speak when we vote, and we do. But we must also give our best effort to encourage the repair of a very broken system. We must do both.

And the courts and prosecutors in government have a role, too. If Attorney General Reno would properly enforce the federal bribery statute, we would see lobbyists and elected officials dragged from the Capitol Building and the White House, their wrists tied, not ours. I would be home in New Hampshire, happily applauding the television news as my government cleaned its own house. In my 90 years, this is the first time I have been arrested. I risk my good name for I do indeed care what my neighbors think about me.

But, Your Honor, some of us do not have much power, except to put our bodies in the way of an injustice to picket, to walk, or to just stand in the way. It will not change the world overnight, but it is all we can do. So I am here today while others block the halls with their corruption. Twenty-five million dollars are changing hands this very evening at a fundraiser down the street. It is the corrupt sale of public policy, and everyone knows it. I would refer those officials and those lobbyists, Your Honor, to Mr. Bob Dylan's advice when he wrote: "Come senators, congressmen, please heed the call. Don't stand in the doorway, don't block up the hall."

Your Honor, the song was a few years early, but the time has now come for change. The times are changing because they must. And they will sweep away the old politician, the self-serving, the self-absorbed, the corrupt. The time of that leader is rapidly fading. We have come through a brief time when we have allowed ourselves to be entertained by corrupt and hapless leaders because they offer so little else, and because, as citizens, we have been priced out of participation and can only try to get some enjoyment out of their follies. But the earth itself can no longer afford them. We owe this change to our children and our grandchildren and our great grandchildren. We need have no fear that a self-governing people can creatively and effectively address their needs as a nation and a world if the corrupt and greedy are out of their way, and ethical leadership is given the helm.

Your Honor, to the business at hand: the old woman who stands before you was arrested for reading the Declaration of Independence in America's Capitol Building. I did not raise my voice to do so and I blocked no hall. But if it is a crime to read the Declaration of Independence in our great hall, then I am guilty.

Thank you very much.

The judge, Chief Judge Hamilton of D.C. federal district court, was silent after Doris made her statement. In sentencing, he said to Doris and the demonstrators (this is an approximate statement until the court transcript becomes available): "Sometimes some people are ahead of the law. It will  change, catching up to where they are. In the meantime, some people like you have to act on behalf of the silent masses." He went on for several minutes with a beautiful statement. He could have imposed sentences of six months imprisonment and $500. Instead, he reduced everyone's sentence to time already served, plus $10.

He met with Doris in his chambers after the session and told her to "take care, because it is people like you who will help us reach our destiny." Some of his clerks were in tears at the conclusion of her heartfelt message and her display of passionate patriotism.[4]

# A Canadian's View of America

There is a man I came to admire recently. I never met him, never heard his broadcasts, because he worked for over 40 years in Canada. His name was Gordon Sinclair.

Mr. Sinclair was a man known to "tell it like it is." And I admire anyone who isn't sensitive to the issue of political correctness. I think that term is ridiculous because I was raised to believe there were only two things in life's path — right or wrong — period.

I try to be truthful in all my daily endeavors, and those who know me say I indeed speak my mind. I'm sorry I never got to meet Gordon Sinclair because I know I would have liked him. He was a colorful figure in 20th century journalism. For nearly five decades he produced a daily radio series called "Let's Be Personal." He gained a reputation for honesty and became popular to millions of listeners. Sinclair is especially remembered for a broadcast he made praising the United States on June 5, 1973. The text of that broadcast, known as "The Americans" is widely circulated on the Internet and I will include it here because he understood much of what many Americans don't.

On June 5, 1973, Gordon Sinclair sat up in bed in Toronto and turned on his TV set. The United States had just pulled out of the Vietnam war, which had ended in a stalemate — a war fought daily on TV, over the radio, and in the press. The aftermath of that war resulted in a worldwide sell-off of American investments. Prices tumbled; the United States economy was in trouble. The war had also divided the American people. At home and abroad, it seemed everyone was lambasting the United States.

He turned on his radio, twisted the dial, and turned it off. He picked up the morning paper. In print, he saw in headlines what he had found on TV and radio — the Americans were taking a verbal beating from nations around the world. Disgusted with what he saw and heard, he was outraged! At 10:30, he walked into his office and "dashed off" two pages in 20 minutes for "Let's Be Personal" for the 11:45 a.m. broadcast. He then turned to writing his 11:50 newscast that was to follow. At 12:01 p.m., the script for "Let's Be Personal" was dropped on the desk of his secretary, who scanned the pages for a suitable heading and then wrote "Americans" across the top and filed it away. The phones were already ringing off the hook.

Here is the text of his views on our beloved country:

**"Let's Be Personal"**
Broadcast June 5, 1973, CFRB, Toronto, Ontario
**Topic: "The Americans"**

The United States dollar took another pounding on German, French, and British exchanges this morning, hitting the lowest point ever known in West Germany. It has declined there by 41 percent since 1971, and this Canadian thinks it is time to speak up for the Americans as the most generous, and possibly the least-appreciated, people in all the earth.

As long as 60 years ago, when I first started to read newspapers, I read of floods on the Yellow River and the Yangtze. Who rushed in with men and money to help? The Americans did.

They have helped control floods on the Nile, the Amazon, the Ganges, and the Niger. Today, the rich bottomland of the Mississippi is under water and no foreign land has sent a dollar to help. Germany, Japan, and, to a lesser extent, Britain and Italy, were lifted out of the debris of war by the Americans who poured in billions of dollars and forgave

*Gordon Sinclair*

other billions in debts. None of those countries is today paying even the interest on its remaining debts to the United States.

When the franc was in danger of collapsing in 1956, it was the Americans who propped it up, and their reward was to be insulted and swindled on the streets of Paris. I was there. I saw it.

When distant cities are hit by earthquakes, it is the United States that hurries in to help . . . Managua, Nicaragua, is one of the most recent examples. So far this spring, 59 American communities have been flattened by tornadoes. Nobody has helped.

The Marshall Plan — the Truman Policy — all pumped billions upon billions of dollars into discouraged countries. Now, newspapers in those countries are writing about the decadent war-mongering Americans. I'd like to see one of those countries that is gloating over the erosion of the United States dollar build its own airplanes. Come on . . . let's hear it! Does any other country in the world have a plane to equal the Boeing Jumbo Jet, the Lockheed Tri-star, or the Douglas DC 10? If so, why don't they fly them? Why do all international lines except Russia fly American planes? Why does no other land on earth even consider putting a man or woman on the moon?

You talk about Japanese technocracy, and you get radios. You talk about German technocracy, and you get automobiles. You talk about American technocracy, and you find men on the moon, not once, but several times . . . and safely home again. You talk about scandals, and the Americans put theirs right in the store window for everyone to see. Even the draft dodgers are not pursued and hounded. They are here on our streets, and most of them, unless they are breaking Canadian laws, are getting American dollars from Ma and Pa at home to spend here.

When the Americans get out of this bind — as they will — who could blame them if they said "the hell with the rest of the world. Let someone else buy the Israel bonds. Let someone else build or repair foreign dams or design foreign buildings that won't shake apart in earthquakes." When the railways of France, Germany, and India were breaking down through age, it was the Americans who rebuilt them. When the Pennsylvania Railroad and the New York Central went broke, nobody loaned them an old caboose. Both are still broke. I can name to you 5,000 times when the Americans raced to the help of other people in trouble.

Can you name me even one time when someone else raced to the Americans in trouble? I don't think there was outside help even during the San Francisco earthquake. Our neighbors have faced it alone and I am one Canadian who is damned tired of hearing them kicked around. They will come out of this thing with their flag high. And when they do, they are entitled to thumb their nose at the lands that are gloating over their present troubles. I hope Canada is not one of these. But there are many smug, self-righteous Canadians. And finally, the American Red Cross was told at its 48th annual meeting in New Orleans this morning that it was broke.

This year's disasters, with the year less than half-over . . . has taken it all and nobody . . . but nobody . . . has helped.[5]

Gordon Sinclair could not have written a book that could have had a greater impact on the world than his two-page script for "The Americans." A book should have been written on the events that followed. But no one, including Sinclair himself, could have envisioned the reaction of the people of the United States — from presidents, state governors, Congress, the Senate, all media including TV, radio, newspapers, magazines, and from the "ordinary" American on the street. Nor could have the Canadian government — stunned by the response to what has come to be regarded as one of Canada's greatest public relations feats in the history of relations with the United States of America.

But, how did Sinclair's tribute to Americans reach them? It had been swept across the United States at the speed of a prairie fire by American radio stations. First, a station in Buffalo called and asked to be fed a tape copy of the broadcast with permission to use — both freely given. Nearby American stations obtained copies from Buffalo or called direct. By the time it reached the Washington, D.C. area, a station had superimposed Sinc's broadcast over an instrumental version of "Bridge Over Troubled Water," and was repeating it at fixed times several times a day. Congressmen and senators heard it. It was read several times into the Congressional Record. A recording contract was signed. As they were finalizing a contract that would see all royalties which would normally be due Gordon Sinclair be paid (at his request) to the American Red Cross, word was received that an unauthorized record using Sinclair's script, but read by another broadcaster, was already flooding the U.S. market. (Subsequently, on learning that this broadcaster had agreed to turn over his royalties to the Red Cross, no legal action was taken.)

Sinclair's recording of his own work (to which Avco had added a stirring rendition of "The Battle Hymn of the Republic") did finally reach record stores and sold hundreds of thousands of copies, but the potential numbers were depressed by the sale of the infringing record. Other record producers and performers (including Tex Ritter) obtained legal permission to make their own versions. In Ritter's case, because of the first-person style of the script, Tex preceded his performance with a proper credit to Sinclair as the author. The American Red Cross received millions of dollars in royalties, and Gordon Sinclair was present at a special ceremony acknowledging his donation.

Advertisers using print media contacted CFRB for permission to publish the text in a non-commercial manner; industrial plants asked for the right to print the script in leaflet form to hand out to their employees.

Gordon Sinclair received invitations to attend and be honored at many functions in the United States which, by number and due to family health problems at the time, he had to decline. However, CFRB newscaster Charles Doering was flown to Washington to give a public reading of "The Americans" to the 28th National Convention of the United States Air Force Association, held September 18, 1974, at the Sheraton Park Hotel. His presentation was performed with the onstage backing of the U.S. Air Force Concert Band, joined by the 100-voice Singing Sergeants in a special arrangement of "The Battle Hymn of the Republic."

Eight years after the first broadcast of "The Americans," President Ronald Reagan made his first official visit to Canada. At the welcoming ceremonies on Parliament Hill, the new president praised "the Canadian journalist who wrote that (tribute) to the United States when it needed a friend." Prime Minister Pierre Trudeau had Sinclair flown to Ottawa to be his guest at the reception that evening.

Sinc had a long and pleasant conversation with Mr. Reagan. The President told him that he had a copy of the record of "The Americans" at his California ranch home when he was governor of the state, and played it from time to time when things looked gloomy.

On the evening of May 15, 1984, following a regular day's broadcasting, Gordon Sinclair suffered a heart attack. He died on May 17. As the word of his illness spread throughout the United States, calls inquiring about his condition were received from as far away as Texas. The editorial in the *Sarasota Herald-Tribune* of May 28 was typical of the reaction of the United States news media — "A Good Friend Passes On."

U.S. President Ronald Reagan: "I know I speak for all Americans in saying the radio editorial Gordon wrote in 1973 praising the accomplishments of the United States was a wonderful inspiration. It was not only critics abroad who forgot this nation's many great achievements, but even critics here at home. Gordon Sinclair reminded us to take pride in our nation's fundamental values." Former Prime Minister

Pierre Trudeau: "Gordon Sinclair's death ends one of the longest and most remarkable careers in Canadian journalism. His wit, irreverence, bluntness, and off-beat views have been part of the media landscape for so long that many Canadians had come to believe he would always be there."

Following a private family service, two thousand people from all walks of life filled Nathan Phillips Square in front of Toronto's City Hall for a public service of remembrance organized by Mayor Art Eggleton. Dignitaries joining him on the platform were Ontario Lieutenant Governor John Black Aird; the premier of Ontario, William Davis; and Metro Chairman Paul Godfrey. Tens of thousands more joined them through CFRB's live broadcast of the service which began symbolically at 11:45 — the regular time of Sinc's daily broadcast of "Let's Be Personal." As Ontario Premier William Davis said of him, "The name could become the classic definition of a full life."[6]

# Tie A Yellow Ribbon

**M**ention the title, and people automatically think of Tony Orlando's hit song. Why? Because it epitomizes the word "freedom." When Tony recorded the hit back in the '70s, nobody expected it to become a mega-hit, let alone an icon. But it did both, big time.

In a very dramatic event, Orlando was asked to sing his famous song to all the returning POWs from Vietnam. As 25,000 cheered and tears flowed freely, Tony sang to the returning heroes.

Today, Tony and his lovely wife, Francine, live in Branson atop a beautiful hillside overlooking Table Rock Lake. The house is just what you might expect from a super star — large, filled with expensive furnishings, and walls covered with gold records and memorabilia from over 40 years in show business. But there is something else inside the Orlando home: unqualified love and respect.

I first met Tony nearly ten years ago when we first opened our show in Branson. His operations manager, Bob Honn, had befriended Shari and me a few days earlier when I stopped to admire his new Chevy Blazer. Bob Honn is just one of those guys you like the moment you meet him. My manager in New York, Ben Carrizzo, had worked with Tony in the past, so naturally we all wanted to see Tony's show at his new Yellow Ribbon Theatre. We weren't disappointed. The nearly 2,000 people

*Dinner at the Radford's — Tony Orlando, Mike, and Jimmie "Honeycomb" Rodgers*

in the audience were treated to a show that pulled out all the stops — countless standing ovations and cheers so loud it made your ears ring. It was wonderful. And now, years later, Tony and Frannie continue to promote and celebrate veterans everywhere they go. "Tie a Yellow Ribbon" has evolved from simple lyrics into a way of life for the Orlandos — true lovers of freedom and the men and women who gave so much.

There are countless stories that I could tell about his patriotism, but Tony chooses to do his "thing" quietly and without fanfare. He believes, as I do, that our veterans are the true heroes of our society and our job is to spread the word.

# We Need More Reporters Like Nick

There aren't many news reporters who are willing to go against whatever is a current popular "cause" and be castigated for being insensitive. We tip our hats to Mr. Gholson. And a special thanks to the *Times Record News* for allowing me to share this story with you. When I called the newsroom recently, a friendly reporter named Bruce Smith took my call. "Just make sure you give the paper and Nick a good plug in your book," he said. I promised I would, so here it is, and now, on with the story.

From the *Times Record News*, Wichita Falls, Texas:

### So Sue Me!

#### by Nick Gholson

Some people, it seems, get offended way too easily. I mean, isn't that what all this prayer hullabaloo is all about — people getting offended? Those of us in the majority are always tippy-toeing around, trying to make sure we don't step on the toes or hurt the feelings of the humorless. And you can bet there's a lawyer standing on every corner making sure we don't. Take this prayer deal. It's absolutely ridiculous. Some atheist goes to a high school football game, hears a kid say a short prayer before the game, and gets offended. So he hires a lawyer and goes to court and asks somebody to pay him a whole bunch of money for all the damage done to him. You would have thought the kid kicked him in the crotch. Damaged for life by a 30-second prayer?

Am I missing something here? I don't believe in Santa Claus, but I'm not going to sue somebody for singing a Ho-Ho-Ho song in December. I don't agree with Darwin, but I didn't go out and hire a lawyer when my high school teacher taught his theory of evolution. Life, liberty, or your pursuit of happiness will not be endangered because someone says a 30-second prayer before a football game. So what's the big deal? It's not like somebody is up there reading the entire Book of Acts. They're just talking to a God they believe in and asking Him to grant safety to the players on the field and the fans going home from the game. "But it's a Christian prayer," some will argue. Yes, and this is the United States of America, a country founded on Christian principles. And we are in the Bible belt. According to our very own phone book, Christian churches outnumber all others better than 200-to-1. So what would you expect — somebody chanting Hare Krishna? If I went to a football game in Jerusalem, I would expect to hear a Jewish prayer. If I went to a soccer game in Baghdad, I would expect to hear a Muslim prayer. If I went to a ping pong match in China, I would expect to hear someone pray to Buddha. And I wouldn't be offended. It wouldn't bother me one bit. When in Rome. . . .

"But what about the atheists?" is another argument. What about them? Nobody is asking them to be baptized. We're not going to pass the collection plate. Just humor us for 30 seconds. If that's asking too much, bring a Walkman or a pair of ear plugs. Go to the bathroom. Visit the concession stand. Call your lawyer. Unfortunately, one or two will make that call. One or two will tell thousands what they can and cannot do. I don't think a short prayer at a football game is going to shake the world's foundations. Nor do I believe that not praying will result in more serious injuries on the field or more fatal car crashes after the game. In fact, I'm not so sure God would even be at all these games if He didn't have to be. Christians are just sick and tired of turning the other cheek while our courts strip us of all our rights. Our parents and grandparents taught us to pray before eating, to pray before we go to sleep. Our Bible tells us just to pray without ceasing. Now a handful of people and their lawyers are telling us to cease praying. God, help us. And if that last sentence offends you — well, just sue me.[7]

# The Great State of Kansas

S enator Bob Dole is a gentleman from Kansas who attained all but the highest office in our land. But did you ever consider what influenced him most and what circumstances propelled him to the heights of political success? How he became the statesman, the past presidential candidate, is the stuff of a true legend. How he did it is, in my opinion, a combination of influences — his belief in God and his family who stood behind him when he left for WWII and stood beside him when he returned with near fatal battle injuries. Another part of his make-up was carved by the values his country was known for — duty, honor, service.

What is it about Kansas and it's citizenry that seems to always stand firm for old-fashioned patriotism? I think the following story helps to answer the question.

When Minister Joe Wright was asked to open the new session of the Kansas Senate in 1999, everyone was expecting the same style, the usual politically correct generalities, but what they heard was a stirring prayer delivered with passion calling our country to repentance and righteousness. The response was instantaneous. A number of legislators walked out during the prayer in protest. In six short weeks, the Central Christian

Church had logged more than 5,000 phone calls with only 47 of those calls responding negatively. The church is now receiving international requests for copies of the prayer from every point on the globe. In fact, Paul Harvey aired the prayer and "The Rest of the Story" on his radio broadcasts, receiving a larger response to it than for any other story he has reported.

The Prayer:

Heavenly Father, we come before You today to ask Your forgiveness and seek Your direction and guidance. We know Your Word says, "Woe on those who call evil good," but that's exactly what we have done. We have lost our spiritual equilibrium and reversed our values.

We confess that:

We have ridiculed the absolute truth of Your Word and called it moral pluralism.

We have worshiped other gods and called it multiculturalism.

We have endorsed perversion and called it an alternative lifestyle.

We have exploited the poor and called it the lottery.

We have neglected the needy and called it self-preservation.

We have rewarded laziness and called it welfare.

We have killed our unborn and called it choice.

We have shot abortionists and called it justifiable.

We have neglected to discipline our children and called it building self-esteem.

We have abused power and called it political savvy.

We have coveted our neighbor's possessions and called it
      ambition.
We have polluted the air with profanity and pornography
      and called it freedom of expression.
We have ridiculed the time-honored values of our forefathers
      and called it enlightenment.
Search us, O God, and know our hearts today;
      try us and see if there be some wicked way in us;
      cleanse us from every sin and set us free.
Guide and bless these men and women who have
      been sent here by the people of Kansas, and who
      have been ordained by you, to direct this great state.
Grant them your wisdom to rule and may their decisions
      direct us to the center of your will. I ask it in the
      name of your Son, the living Savior, Jesus Christ.
Amen.[8]

Kansas has much for which to be proud. Thank you, Joe Wright for setting an example for us to follow.

As many of you know, Col. Bob Patrick and Senator Dole asked me to spearhead the fundraising efforts in Branson to help build the WWII Memorial in Washington, D.C. It was an honor to be a part of the team responsible for paying tribute to the "Greatest Generation."

It isn't an accident that one of Kansas's most loved sons led the effort.

**SENATOR BOB DOLE**
901 15TH STREET, N.W.
SUITE 410
WASHINGTON, D.C. 20005

August 16, 1999

Mr. Mike Radford
*Remember When* Theater
3562 Shepherd of the Hills Expressway
Branson, MO 65616

Dear Mike:

Thanks so much for your book. It really took me back to the days of fond memories and simpler times when God, family and country was the bedrock we all stood on. If your show is anything like your book, I am certain it is a winner as well.

I understand you give veterans, especially World War II veterans, a moving tribute during each of your shows. I commend you for doing this. We need to take every opportunity we can to say "Thank You" to all those who served and sacrificed so magnificently during World War II, as well as other conflicts. You are setting an outstanding example that all America needs to follow.

Thanks also for spearheading Branson's campaign to raise support for the National World War II Memorial. The efforts by the Branson community are sure to put your city on the map as a leading supporter of this long overdue tribute to America's greatest generation.

Again, thank you for everything and may God continue to bless you and your family.

Sincerely,

BOB DOLE

# Two Differing Chicago Legends

This is another of those anonymous stories sent to me over the great information highway. It gives great debate to whether it is our environment or heredity that leads to greatness. These stories certainly contradict each theory. No matter, I know you will enjoy.

*Story number one:*

World War II produced many heroes. One such man was Butch O'Hare. He was a fighter pilot assigned to an aircraft carrier in the South Pacific. One day his entire squadron was sent on a mission. After he was airborne, he looked at his fuel gauge and realized that someone had forgotten to top off his fuel tank. He would not have enough fuel to complete his mission and get back to his ship. His flight leader told him to return to the carrier. Reluctantly he dropped out of formation and headed back to the fleet. As he was returning to the mother ship, he saw something that turned his blood cold, a squadron of Japanese Zeroes was speeding its way toward the American fleet.

The American fighters were gone on a sortie, a mission that left the fleet all but defenseless. He couldn't reach his squadron and bring them back in time to save the fleet. Nor could he warn the fleet of the approaching danger. There was only one thing to do. He must somehow divert them from the fleet. Laying aside all thoughts of personal safety, he dove into the formation of Japanese planes. Wing-mounted 50 calibers blazed as he charged in, attacking one surprised enemy plane and then another. Butch weaved in and out of the now broken formation and fired at as many planes as possible until finally all his ammunition was spent. Undaunted, he continued the assault. He dove at the Zeroes, trying to at least clip off a wing or tail, in hopes of damaging as many enemy planes as possible, rendering them unfit to fly. He was desperate to do anything he could to keep them from reaching the American ships. Finally, the exasperated Japanese squadron took off in another direction.

Deeply relieved, Butch O'Hare and his tattered fighter limped back to the carrier. Upon arrival he reported in and related the event surrounding his return. The film from the camera mounted on his plane told the tale. It showed the extent of Butch's daring attempt to protect his fleet. He was recognized as a hero and given one of the nation's highest military honors. And today, O'Hare Airport in Chicago is named in tribute to the courage of this great man. A real hero — a real patriot.

*Story number two:*

In the gangster days a man called Easy Eddie lived in Chicago. At that time, Al Capone virtually owned the city. Capone wasn't famous for anything heroic. His exploits were anything but praiseworthy. He was, however, notorious for enmeshing the city of Chicago in everything from bootlegged booze and prostitution to murder. Easy Eddie was Capone's lawyer and for a good reason. He was very good! In fact, his skill at legal maneuvering kept Big Al out of jail for a long time. To show his appreciation, Capone paid him very well. Not only was the money big, Eddie got special dividends. For instance, he and his family occupied a fenced-in mansion with live-in help and all of the conveniences of the day. The estate was so large that it filled an entire Chicago city block.

Yes, Eddie lived the high life of the Chicago mob and gave little consideration to the atrocites that went on around him. Eddie did have one soft spot, however. He had a son that he loved dearly. Eddie saw to it that his young son had the best of everything — clothes, cars, and a good education. Nothing was withheld. Price was no object. And, despite his involvement with organized crime, Eddie even tried to teach him right from wrong.

Yes, Eddie tried to teach his son to rise above his own sordid life. He wanted him to be a better man than he was. Yet, with all his wealth and influence, there were two things that Eddie couldn't give his son. Two things Eddie sacrificed to the Capone mob that he could not pass on to his beloved son — a good name and a good example.

One day, Easy Eddie reached a difficult decision. Offering his son a good name was far more important than all the riches he could lavish on him. He had to rectify all the wrong that he had done. He would go to the authorities and tell the truth about Scarface Al Capone. He would try to clean up his tarnished name and offer his son some semblance of integrity. To do this he must testify against the mob, and he knew that the cost would be great. But more than anything, he wanted to be an example to his son. He wanted to do his best to make restoration and, hopefully, have a good name to leave his son. So, he testified. Within the year, Easy Eddie's life ended in a blaze of gunfire on a lonely Chicago street. He had given his son the greatest gift he had to offer at the greatest price he would ever pay.

I know what you're thinking. What do these two stories have to do with one another? Well, you see, Butch O'Hare was Easy Eddie's son. And as Paul Harvey says, "Now, you know the rest of the story."

*Be a legend to your children . . . remember the power of example.*

# Red Skelton — American Patriot

The following words were spoken by the late Red Skelton on his television program as he related the story of his teacher, Mr. Laswell, who felt his students had come to think of the Pledge of Allegiance as merely something to recite in class each day.

I've been listening to you boys and girls recite the Pledge of Allegiance all semester and it seems as though it is becoming monotonous to you. If I may, may I recite it and try to explain to you the meaning of each word?

I — me, an individual, a committee of one.

PLEDGE — dedicate all of my worldly goods to give without self pity.

ALLEGIANCE — my love and my devotion.

TO THE FLAG — our standard, Old Glory, a symbol of freedom. Wherever she waves, there's respect because your loyalty has given her a dignity that shouts freedom is everybody's job!

UNITED — that means that we have all come together.

STATES — individual communities that have united into 48

*Red Skelton*

great states. Forty-eight individual communities with pride and dignity and purpose; all divided with imaginary boundaries, yet united to a common purpose, and that's love for country.

AND TO THE REPUBLIC — a state in which sovereign power is invested in representatives chosen by the people to govern. And government is the people and it's from the people to the leaders, not from the leaders to the people.

FOR WHICH IT STANDS, ONE NATION — one nation, meaning "so blessed by God."

INDIVISIBLE — incapable of being divided.

WITH LIBERTY — which is freedom — the right of power to live one's own life without threats, fear, or some sort of retaliation.

AND JUSTICE — the principle or quality of dealing fairly with others.

FOR ALL — which means, boys and girls, it's as much your country as it is mine.

And now, let me hear you recite the Pledge of Allegiance:

I pledge allegiance to the flag of the United States of America, and to the republic, for which it stands; one nation, indivisible, with liberty and justice for all.

Since I was a small boy, two states have been added to our country and two words have been added to the Pledge of Allegiance . . . UNDER GOD.

Wouldn't it be a pity if someone said that is a prayer and that would be eliminated from schools, too?

— Red Skelton

*A true American hero, Gen. Paul Tibbets, pilot of the*
Enola Gay, *which dropped the bomb ending WWII*

# SECTION FOUR

## *Role Models*

# *Fifties Role Models*

After performing our "Remember When Show" one day, I had the chance to chat with a little lady from Ohio. I asked what she would change in American culture today. Her answer was swift and to the point — she wished today's kids could see the same clean and wholesome movies she grew up watching back in the '40s and '50s.

Back then, our role models never got arrested, and moms and dads across the USA never worried about their kids on weekends, because the Saturday matinee was the coolest place to be and the theater ushers and staff always cared for the kids and made sure everyone was okay.

Yep, when I was growing up in the '50s, there were two people most kids pretended to "be." We'd jump on our stick ponies and ride out behind the barn to look for those make-believe bad guys we knew were always hiding along the trail, waiting to bushwhack us little buckaroos. The two movie stars we "became" were Roy Rogers and Dale Evans. I loved Roy and Dale with all my heart, and I still do! They taught us right from wrong and always defended the helpless.

I wear a Roy Rogers wrist watch. I do it because each time I look to see the time, I see my hero standing next to his wife, Dale. Silly? Nostalgic? Yes, it is. The reason I wear a Roy Rogers wrist watch is that when I glance at it, I am reminded of the kind of man I strive to be. A

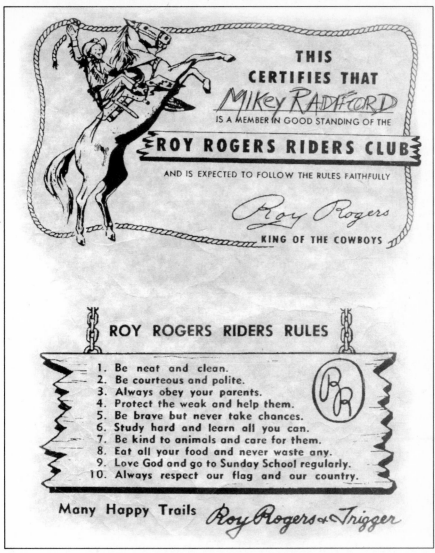

THIS
CERTIFIES THAT
*Mikey Radford*
IS A MEMBER IN GOOD STANDING OF THE

**ROY ROGERS RIDERS CLUB**

AND IS EXPECTED TO FOLLOW THE RULES FAITHFULLY

*Roy Rogers*

KING OF THE COWBOYS

**ROY ROGERS RIDERS RULES**

1. Be neat and clean.
2. Be courteous and polite.
3. Always obey your parents.
4. Protect the weak and help them.
5. Be brave but never take chances.
6. Study hard and learn all you can.
7. Be kind to animals and care for them.
8. Eat all your food and never waste any.
9. Love God and go to Sunday School regularly.
10. Always respect our flag and our country.

**Many Happy Trails** *Roy Rogers & Trigger*

*Simple common sense rules that built character*

loyal husband. A good role model. Successful. A passionate patriot. All descriptions of the man who influenced millions of us "boomers."

Yes, I feel sad for kids today because they don't have the kind of role models we did back when we were young. America needs people like them more than ever because they stood for everything that was good

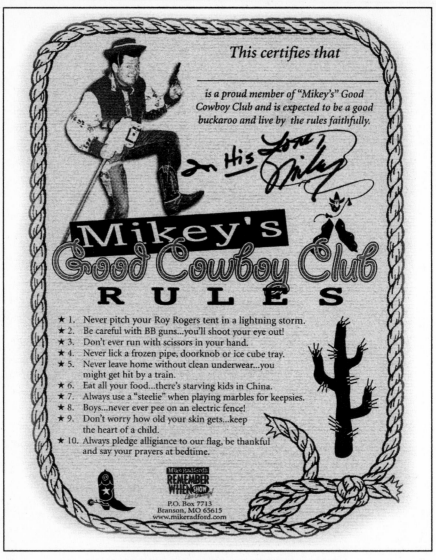

*This certifies that*

_____

*is a proud member of "Mikey's" Good Cowboy Club and is expected to be a good buckaroo and live by the rules faithfully.*

## Mikey's Good Cowboy Club RULES

★ 1. Never pitch your Roy Rogers tent in a lightning storm.
★ 2. Be careful with BB guns...you'll shoot your eye out!
★ 3. Don't ever run with scissors in your hand.
★ 4. Never lick a frozen pipe, doorknob or ice cube tray.
★ 5. Never leave home without clean underwear...you might get hit by a train.
★ 6. Eat all your food...there's starving kids in China.
★ 7. Always use a "steelie" when playing marbles for keepsies.
★ 8. Boys...never ever pee on an electric fence!
★ 9. Don't worry how old your skin gets...keep the heart of a child.
★ 10. Always pledge alligiance to our flag, be thankful and say your prayers at bedtime.

Mike Radford's
REMEMBER WHEN SHOW
P.O. Box 7713
Branson, MO 65615
www.mikeradford.com

*In 1994, Roy Roger's family gave permission
for Mike to create his own version.*

and unsoiled in our nation. The simple but poignant example of Roy Rogers' philosophy taught us kids right from wrong.

Recently, a man from Michigan told me about how he patterned his life after one of his childhood heroes and went on to finish medical school. His hero was his dad. So you see not all our heroes were up on the silver screen or playing in Yankee Stadium. No, the real heroes are the moms and dads, the grandfathers and grandmas who show us how to live with dignity and grace. It's their examples of old-fashioned patriotism and polite manners that we need to teach to today's youth. That's why our old-time role models were so good for us. There was no gray area — we all knew the difference between right and wrong. Today the lines are so blurry a kid can't figure out what is right and wrong.

Back in the '30s, '40s, and '50s, when the movie was over, "THE END" came on the screen. It was the guy in the white hat who always got the girl, while the bad guys in the black hats always went to the "pokey."

Thinking back to those days, I remember how patriotic our teachers were. In February, or during a president's birthday, our classroom assignments always revolved around essays and book reports about the presidents.

*Mike joins Roy Rogers Jr. on his radio show.*

Remember cutting silhouettes of their heads and stapling them all around the classroom? When I was a kid in the '50s, we always celebrated Dwight David Eisenhower's birthday in October. His birthday was easy for me to remember because many important things happened on that day,

*Mary Eisenhower (Ike's granddaughter) tours Mike's Hall of Heroes.*

the 14th of October. It was President Eisenhower's birthday; it was the day Chuck Yeager became the first pilot to break the sound barrier and live to tell about it. Then on October 14, 1964, a young United States Marine, Lt. Billy Mills, shocked the Olympic world by winning the gold medal in the 10,000 meters. Oh, and one other great event took place on October 14. Just like Chuck Yeager, I too "broke" the sound barrier! It's the day I was born in 1946!

My first memories of patriotic celebration began when I was around five years old. My grandpa Mitch was a veteran of WWI and I remember sitting on his knee as he tried to teach me to speak the very limited Italian and French he'd picked up while fighting in the trenches in Europe. Once in a while I would see his eyes seem to lose focus as his mind wandered somewhere. The normal relaxed features of his face would often harden. Then with a shake of his head, he would return back to me sitting on his leg. Back then our family was mostly Democrats. Even for a youngster like me, it was fun watching Harry Truman occasionally rant and rave on Grandpa's old black and white television set. Grandpa used to tell me to watch President Truman, to learn from him and be honest and always say what's on my mind. I guess without knowing it, Mr. Truman became an early influence on my character, too. "Give'm hell, Harry!" Grandpa Mitch would shout, fist shaking high above his head. Whenever he got too upset about something on television, Grandma Harriet would yell from out in the kitchen, "Now calm down, Mitch! You mustn't talk like that in front of Mikey!" She'd then return to her kitchenly duties, whistling her happy tunes. Yes, school days were different then. When I was a kid, history was a subject most teachers seemed to be interested in — we were all proud Americans back then.

The events in New York, Washington, and in the skies of Pennsylvania changed every one of us in deep, lasting ways. We are now keenly aware of what happens when apathy diminishes our judgment and the enemy silently creeps into our camp. We must always remember.

*Mike co-hosting on PBS during WWII special*

# Dr. Martin Luther King

August 28, 1963 (excerpt)

I say to you today, my friends, that in spite of the difficulties and frustrations of the moment, I still have a dream. It is a dream deeply rooted in the American dream.

I have a dream that one day this nation will rise up and live out the true meaning of its creed: "We hold these truths to be self-evident: that all men are created equal." I have a dream that one day on the red hills of Georgia, the sons of former slaves and the sons of former slave-owners will be able to sit down together at a table of brotherhood. I have a dream that one day, even the state of Mississippi, a desert state, sweltering with the heat of injustice and oppression, will be transformed into an oasis of freedom and justice. I have a dream that my four children will one day live in a nation where they will not be judged by the color of their skin but by the content of their character. I have a dream today. . . .

I have a dream that one day every valley shall be exalted, every hill and mountain shall be made low, the rough places will be made plain, and the crooked places will be made straight, and the glory of the Lord shall be revealed, and all flesh shall see it together. This is our hope. This is the faith with which I return to the South. With this faith we will be able to hew out of the mountain of despair a stone of hope. With this faith we will be able to transform the jangling discords of our nation into a beautiful symphony of brotherhood. With this faith we will be able to work together, to pray together, to struggle together, to go to jail together, to stand up for freedom together, knowing that we will be free one day.

This will be the day when all of God's children will be able to sing with new meaning, "My country 'tis of thee, sweet land of liberty, of thee I sing. Land where my fathers died, land of the pilgrim's pride, from every mountainside, let freedom ring." And if America is to be a great nation, this must become true. So let freedom ring from the . . . mighty mountains of New York. Let freedom ring from the heightening Alleghenies of Pennsylvania! Let freedom ring from the snowcapped Rockies of Colorado! Let freedom ring from the curvaceous peaks of California! But not only that; let freedom ring from Stone Mountain of Georgia! Let freedom ring from Lookout Mountain of Tennessee! Let freedom ring from every hill and molehill of Mississippi. From every mountainside, let freedom ring.

When we let freedom ring, when we let it ring from every village and every hamlet, from every state and every city, we will be able to speed up that day when all of God's children, black men and white men, Jews and Gentiles, Protestants and Catholics, will be able to join hands and sing in the words of the old Negro spiritual, "Free at last! free at last! thank God Almighty, we are free at last!"

# How to Save the Next Generation — Bring Back the Draft

Time is a peculiar thing. It seems to evaporate like beads of water dancing on a wood-burning stove.

Wasn't it "yesterday" we witnessed the horrors of 9-11? In many ways, our collective "lifetime" has been just as transitory with more drama than our forefathers could ever imagine, or have endured. Americans live with a culture of our own creation and wonder how we allowed ourselves to be dragged down to the moral levels we now ask our children to live. We are not the same nation or individuals we once were. The evil that attacked our homeland has changed us forever. Patriotism was reborn on that day — a newly discovered emotion born in the hearts of millions of people who, 24 hours before, were apathetic toward anything that rang of flag waving. Everything changed in a New York minute.

The WWII generation had the distinction of having GIs return from war who were greeted with flag-waving folks singing "God Bless America." Our generation, called "baby-boomers," answered the call to serve in Vietnam, and most did so with honor. Why then were these patriotic kids so mistreated upon setting foot back home in the USA? Why were they advised to change into "civvies" (civilian clothes) so the angry mobs of university elitists wouldn't spit on them as they disembarked at airline terminals or bus stations. A sad fact of life in 2004 is that many of these unpatriotic elitists, the very ones who showered spit upon our returning sons and daughters, are now teaching in many universities, spewing their socialist propaganda on the Vietnam veterans' grandchildren. This is one of life's cruel ironies. If it were possible to turn back the hands of time, how do you think today's United States would look if *every* able-bodied man and woman had to complete at least two years in the service of their country? So instead of being protected by advantages of educational status or wealth, every child had to perform some kind of service to our society. Hasn't it been said, "Nothing is free. Somebody paid for it."

In 1999, I wrote an article which not one newspaper would print. As I re-read the article in consideration of including it in this book, I realized the reason why. The title itself paints a vivid picture of how different society is today, and how the left political agenda has destroyed much of the moral fabric our founders created. Here now is the article I submitted two years *before* 9-11-01.

## It Begins:

We as a nation desperately need to change our boys into men, girls into women; and the time has come to do something about it. Bringing back the draft would revitalize America and cause changes desperately needed in our society. I know the idea doesn't have a July snowball's chance in Arizona, but it is essential if we are to save our younger generation. We are a nation filled with millions of fat, lazy, rude, and sugar-addicted kids who complain they are bored all the time. Helping around the house is too difficult for their delicate little bodies and they whine every time their parents demand they do something as laborious as taking

out the trash. Well, I have the answer, kids! Let's bring back the draft! Oh, I can hear the moans and groans right now. Maybe a course should be added to every classroom in America; let's call it, "By the way, freedom is not free."

Now, I know the dumbest things offend some folks, so I'd better apologize up front for offending some of you. For instance, let's take the phrase "political correctness." I'd love to meet the moron who came up with that one. Why do they think we have to kowtow to this group or that? If we don't phrase our sentences to please them, or pander to *their* agenda we are called racists or worse. Come on, whatever happened to the common sense values we learned as kids.

But wait! I just realized that not all Americans were lucky enough to be raised in the '30s, '40s, '50s, and even the '60s. And that is a shame, because being a kid in those days meant learning things like, "Yes sir, no sir," and, "Yes ma'am, no ma'am." I would nearly faint if some of the rowdy little creeps I've witnessed in shopping malls actually showed respect for their parents. And imagine if they had to actually get off their fat keisters to help out around the house! These days, I watch some kids and shake my head because not all, but some, need a good spanking for the disrespect and rudeness they show their parents. Oops, that isn't politically correct. So what? It's time people take a look at how far down the ladder we have allowed our moral base to slip.

Everyone abhors child abuse, but come on, I'm talking about old-fashioned discipline. When I was "little Mikey" and was a good boy, I got dessert. On those occasions when I was naughty, guess what? I got my little caboose warmed up! Never once did I think it was child abuse. I knew I was swatted because I broke the rules. The common sense of it is staggering; I hate to shock some of you, but that's how kids learn right from wrong. Rudeness and moral decay are rampant, but I have an idea that at least gives today's kids some chance of finding their direction and purpose for living and at the very least would give a rebirth of patriotism not seen in decades. What's my solution? Bring back the draft!

Now before some of you go nuts on me, I am not referring to building a vast war machine. And that brings another thought to mind. America has NEVER been an aggressor toward another freedom-loving nation. We at times have been forced into the role of liberator which is a far cry from invader. I've given a lot of thought to the notion, and here is why I believe America would be restored if every young man and woman gave two years of service to his or her country. It's a small price to pay for the blessings many kids today take for granted. Let me carry you back to what I experienced when I was drafted in my freshman year of college. Reporting for basic training is a day forever in my memory, a day unlike any other before or since.

## Dateline 1966, Ft. Polk, Louisiana

Like millions of American kids before me, I was forced to get up much earlier than I wanted. But then, I was about to experience lots of things I didn't ask for or want. The alarm shattered my last night's sleep and forced me to catch the Greyhound bus that would whisk this 18-year-old kid off into a world of which I had no clue what awaited me. As the bus slowly turned out of the station, I strained to look out the steamy window and watched my parents wave goodbye. My stepdad had a slight, albeit knowing, smile; Mom waved her tatted hankie as tears trickled down her cheek. Settling back in the seat I wondered what awaited me. Would I have to go to Vietnam? Or would the many letters the Major League scouts wrote for me change my destiny and keep me from harm's way?

Long and uncomfortable hours passed, filled with reminiscences of my childhood — playing baseball from sunrise to sunset, building tree houses, and sleeping outside in the warmth of the summer nights gazing at millions of twinkling stars that God hung in the night sky. Thoughts of high school days and the fun we had as kids — then in the middle of my reminiscence, occasional fear entered and gripped my heart. Then more mind-dulling hours as endless miles passed beneath me. In what seemed like minutes, the bus jerked to a stop. Suddenly the door flew open and a crazed army drill sergeant jumped into the aisle shouting at the top of his lungs, "Alright you scum bags! Get outa your seats! Get up! Up! Up . . . and I mean NOW!"

In shock, we all jumped to our feet and flew down the steps as our tormentor ordered us to get into a straight line. Confusion and fear reigned supreme, for no one had ever treated us like this before. Trying to comply with his orders, I stood rigid as the bully in the Smoky-the-Bear hat swaggered toward me. Suddenly, the brim of his hat was bouncing off my forehead. The drill sergeant in camouflage fatigues stared at me, his eyes narrowing into tiny slits. I remember thinking it was silly to be playing "stare down" at this age. Those of you who know me understand I have a rather large sense of humor and on occasion find it hard to be serious. This was a moment I knew comedy had no place, but I couldn't stop the tiny grin developing in the corner of my mouth. The rock solid brim of the drill sergeant's hat began to bounce harder against my forehead.

"Something funny to you scum bag?" he shouted.

"Nope," I replied.

"No, SIR, to you maggot! Do I make myself clear, boy?" With his nose pressed firmly on mine he went berserk. Spit was flying out as he screamed, "Whenever I talk to any of you momma's boys, you will AL-WAYS refer to me as 'Drill Sergeant,' your answers will be, 'Yes, sir, or no, sir!' Do you understand, you slimy little maggots!?"

In a scattered, quivering cadence we replied, "Yes, sir, Drill Sergeant!" And so began our journey from sloppy, undisciplined, and sometimes lazy kids into a group of young men who would graduate three months later into a fighting force.

Today's kids could expect pretty much the same "boot camp" adventure. The mental and physical training would transform today's "kids" into men and women, just as in every era before them.

Let's fast forward to boot camp graduation day . . . hmmm, what would we see? How different would today's fat and lazy have become? Let's pretend we are sitting in the reviewing stands as the class of recruits parades before us. Who are these lean young soldiers, sailors, airmen, or marines standing straight as proud patriots? Shoulders rigid, chests stuck out, chiseled jaws set and firm. Could these be the recruits who, a few weeks earlier, had trouble doing one simple push-up? We'd watch as the drill sergeant approaches each, proud of the "soldier" he created. The man who once called them "scum bags" and "maggots" now salutes each saying, "Congratulations, young man (or woman), you are now a member of the United States Armed Services." Right on cue, the new soldier snaps a perfectly executed salute. "Thank you, sir!" he shouts with confidence. Both soldier and mentor exchange a glance known only by men and women who have been there. If you have, you understand the emotion of realizing you are no longer "green" but have evolved into manhood. It's a feeling sadly missed by millions of young Americans today.

Some in our society will claim that this is unfair and we shouldn't demand such discipline from our younger citizens. But have those folks

considered what kind of world we would have today if our parents and grandparents hadn't answered the call? Our ancestors paid the price for freedom, and freedom is NOT free. All gave some, and some gave all.

Okay, if we don't make GIs out of them, let's create some kind of federal service akin to the famous Civilian Conservation Corps implemented by President Franklin D. Roosevelt. Nobody on either side of the aisle in Washington, D.C., will argue the CCC's positive influence. Mandatory service turned our country around and made men of boys and provided critical services needed in our nation at the time. History proves my point. Service to America is a good thing to ask of our young citizens.

Let's look at the scenario in present-day America. Tens of thousands of "Jacks and Jills" would climb aboard Greyhound buses and report for basic training. Twelve weeks later we'd have a whole new generation of doers who are in the best shape of their lives. Physically fit, mentally tough, and ready to serve the country that keeps them free from tyranny. They would have a new respect for those words "yes sir" or "no sir." Something magical takes place inside the hearts of young people when they become a part of something much larger than themselves, something so noble as duty to country. A dramatic transformation takes place when they realize it's their turn to give something back to their nation. They learn that freedom comes with a high price tag and they are reborn in the spirit of patriotism. If you look at today's active-duty personnel, you will see the brightest, most dedicated patriots who ever put on a uniform. They are proud of who they are and what they have become. It's a feeling that only those who've been there understand.

Where's the money coming from to support this ambitious plan? Our friends in Washington, D.C., have lots of dough to throw around.

Hey, I have an idea! Let's stop giving BILLIONS of our dollars to corrupt foreign governments who hate the USA anyway. What a concept! Let's use *our* money to take care of *Americans*. My Grandma Harriet often said, "Family comes first. If we have enough left over, we'll share with our neighbors." That's just plain good old-fashioned U.S. common sense.

Think about it. Millions of American kids would receive good job training. They would learn real-life skills that could garner *real* jobs once they leave the service. The educational and occupational training would remain impossible dreams for some who otherwise stayed in civilian life. Some of the direct benefits our nation could expect would be engineer battalions fixing roads, building homes for the homeless, and building bridges where needed. Military police could be trained and positioned on border patrols to control the millions of illegals streaming into our country. Let's set up neighborhood health clinics manned by the armed services medical corps with doctors, nurses, and specialists who would give two years of their life to making the United States a better place. The United States Air Force could fast track upgrades to obsolete air traffic control systems. Let's allow Marines to win the drug war and stop the drug-runners and dealers poisoning our children. Bring back the draft!

Army chaplain Col. Lamar Hunt told me, *"If a kid says he shouldn't be drafted because he is going to be a minister, then let him do noncombatant work in a hospital chaplain's office or some place equivalent. When a draft means all serve, it's true democracy. But when it means only the poor and unconnected, its elitism at its worst, completely alien to the great ideas of equality under God and the rules of our Founders Constitution."*

Save the next generation — bring back the draft. We would have the manpower to do so much more. Don't we mobilize the National Guard

and Reserves in times of crisis? Well, why wait for a crisis? Is it going to take another Pearl Harbor to awaken our society to the evils that are just waiting to attack us while we sleep? [Remember I wrote this in 1999.] The expanded military service I'm talking about will already have the GIs in place to proactively serve and protect our citizens.

But as with all ambitious plans, there is a downside. The dedicated servicemen and women who have so respectfully served in our volunteer military will have to put up with the ones who think they are above it all. For the good of the many, we have to do it anyway. When I called Col. Bob Patrick (U.S. Army, ret.), one of the leaders building the WWII Memorial in Washington, D.C., he responded, *"My major point is being a part of something bigger than yourself is an important lesson in life. In the military you are taught this lesson from day one when your individuality is stripped away and you are very quickly taught to subordinate yourself to the service you have sworn to undertake — service to your country and its values. It's bewildering at first, but it's an awesome feeling when you come to understand what it's all about."*

Jerry Luedke, a retired Navy man and decorated Vietnam veteran added a unique viewpoint as he remained in the service as a recruiter during the draft era and the transition to the all volunteer service we have today. *"Great idea that will cure a lot of our nation's ills. Every able-bodied man and woman will feel a sense of fulfillment and pride that cannot be obtained in any other way. Serving your country changes young people in deep and lasting ways."*

Army Col. Jim Coy, another highly decorated Vietnam veteran adds, *"I agree with and support the restoration of the draft. I believe every young American should have the opportunity to serve the nation. I also believe that a few young men and women who, because of religious convictions or other strongly held views, believe they could not carry a weapon in the defense of our nation, should also have to serve. I would offer these individuals service in the Peace Corps or in a program similar to the old Vista program."*

The concept excites Senator Dave Zien of Wisconsin, another Vietnam veteran: *"The draft prepares you for life. It would reinforce the moral fabric of our nation and strengthen the heart and soul of our country by giving us a renewed sense of who we are as Americans. Kids today don't get that kind of direction."*

Bring back the draft. We will watch some spoiled kids scream and holler all the way to the airport or bus station. Well, too bad. It'll do more good than they can ever imagine. Want examples? Charissa Cosky was in college when she applied for the Air Force ROTC program. She graduated an officer and served four years of active duty to repay the Air Force for providing her four years of college education. Great deal? You bet. Today Charissa flies a Boeing 777 for United Airlines. Her parents say her successes can be traced directly to the day she began her military service while a young woman in college. Another good example is Ben Hall. He was a young man headed down the wrong road of life until a caring adult pointed him in the right direction — the Marine Corps recruiting station. His young life was a tough one, filled with violence, gangs, and being homeless. The military straightened him out and taught him life-changing values, furnishing Ben with direction and something of which to be proud. Ben now owns a successful business and gives all glory to God *and* the U.S. Marine Corps.

I can just hear the far "lefties" screaming, *"It isn't fair to draft people!"* So what? To revitalize our nation every able-bodied kid needs to serve a two-year hitch. I did it, and looking back it was the best thing that could have happened to me. The military turned me from a cocky kid into a young man who respected authority. It's done all over the world and kids in other countries don't like it either, but they serve. Lt. General Don Parker added, *"Mike, you are a dedicated American patriot and I support your views in this article. However, I seriously doubt any politician will touch this idea with a ten-foot pole. Nevertheless, as a drafted 20 year old during the Korean War who served his country proudly for 39 years, I fully support some type of universal service to our nation. It can best be described as an 'investment' in our nations future."* The general is right. Two years of service won't fix everything, but it will dramatically change one person at a time. After millions of kids have served, we would witness a renewed sense of patriotism as countless young Americans would be proud to be called veterans.

It is a noble thing to have served your country, and if the draft returns, they *will* be proud. It is a right of passage that culminates in changing a boy into a man, a girl into a woman. So I say to the president, congress, and senate, "Help save the next generation . . . bring back the draft."

# SECTION FIVE
## Old-fashioned Values

# I Pledge Allegiance...

When we were attacked on September 11, my wife Shari and I stood in silent disbelief in front of our television. How could this be happening in our nation? Why? How could this happen to us? Like you, we were heartsick and numb. In the days following the tragedy, I kept asking myself, *What good could come from this?* The question kept going through my mind because I believe for every "bad" thing that happens, there is something "good" to be found . . . if we search hard enough. But this was different; nothing like this had ever occurred in my lifetime and I was having a hard time finding any good stemming from the horrors of September 11. One day I realized I had discovered three "good" things that emerged from the rubble:

1. For the first time in 40 years, kids from coast to coast are being allowed to pledge allegiance to the flag of the United States of America.

2. God has been invited back into most school systems.

3. Americans are turning back to old-fashioned values that taught right from wrong — and good from evil.

When I was a little kid growing up in northern California, I remember vividly how proud I felt every morning when our teacher would ask us to stand up and say the Pledge of Allegiance. It wasn't a task we dreaded or moaned about — we were happy to do it. The day wouldn't have started right if we didn't place our hands over our hearts and say those words that meant so much. It unified the classroom. It justified who we were and what our lives were all about. It made us realize we were special. Maybe that explains why so many kids today don't seem to know who they are, or what they stand for. Back in the '30s, '40s, '50s, and '60s we all knew who we were — Americans, and we were darned proud of it, too.

Photo courtesy of the Smalley family

# "Remember Me?"

by David C. Graham

Hello. . . . Remember me? Some people call me Old Glory, others call me the Star Spangled Banner, but whatever they call me, I am your flag, the flag of the United States of America.

Something has been bothering me, so I thought I might talk it over with you — because it is about you and me. I remember some time ago, people would line up on both sides of the street to watch the parade, and naturally I was leading every one, proudly waving in the breeze.

When your daddy saw me coming, he immediately removed his hat and placed it against his left shoulder so that his hand was directly over his heart — remember? And you, I remember, were standing there, straight as a soldier. You didn't have a hat, but you were giving the right salute. Remember your little sister? Not to be outdone, she was saluting the same as you with her right hand over her heart — remember?

What happened? I'm still the same old flag. Oh, I've added a few more stars since those parades of long ago. But now, some-how, I don't feel as proud as I used to feel. When I come down your street, you just stand there with your hands in your pockets. You may give me a small glance, and then you look away. I see children running around you shouting; they don't seem to know who I am.

I saw one man take his hat off, then he looked around and when he didn't see anybody else take off their hat, he quickly put his on again. Is it a sin to be patriotic today? Have you forgotten what I stand for, and where I have been? Anzio, Guadalcanal, Iwo Jima, Korea, Vietnam, and Desert Storm!

Take a look at the memorial honor rolls and see the names

of those patriotic Americans who gave their lives to keep this republic free. When you salute me, you are actually saluting THEM. Well, it won't be long until I'll be coming down your street again. So when you see me, please

*WWII veteran Tim LaHaye, co-author of the "Left Behind" series of books*

stand straight and place your hand over your heart and I'll know
that you remembered . . . and then I'll salute YOU . . . by waving
back."[9]

During the veterans' salute in my Branson show, I read Mr. Graham's words to hopefully spark an interest in this "thing" called patriotism. Too many young people today don't have a clue why we "older"
people are so passionate about the subject. What they don't know could
literally kill them. For when our freedoms are taken away, the indomi-
table human spirit will revolt in protest. It is imperative that we all stand
up for our sovereignty so those who want to eliminate it will know, just
as the British learned, "Don't Tread on Me!"

One man I greatly admire is a Vietnam veteran named Sam Gaskill.
Sam serves in the Missouri House of Representatives and stands proudly

*Former Missouri State Representative Sam Gaskill (veteran F-4 pilot)
with Mike and U.S. Congressman J.C. Watts (ret.)*

for his God, family, and country. We were talking one day about the state of patriotism in America and he told me about a bill he proposed in the Missouri House. Mr. Gaskill's bill says that yes, people have the right to protest and burn the flag as a form of their first amendment right to free speech. His bill says, and I paraphrase, "If I, or any other citizen who loves the Star Spangled Banner catches you doing it . . . we have the right to beat the crap out of you without the threat of legal action against us!"

Thank you, Representative Gaskill, for having the courage to stand up for what is right. I encourage all of you to do the same because millions of men and women died fighting for that flag. Let's honor their memory by protecting it from the idiots who have far too much time on their hands and have no concept of defending the memory of our fallen heroes.

*Mike accepts the Bob Hope Patriot Award at the Congressional Medal of Honor banquet.*

# One Nation Under God

Here's a fascinating tidbit about our currency that I received over the Internet. Again, its author is anonymous. I know you'll be amazed.

Take out a one dollar bill and look at it. The one dollar bill you're looking at first came off the presses in 1957 in its present design. This so-called paper money is, in fact, a cotton and linen blend, with red and blue minute silk fibers running through it. It is actually material. We've all washed it without it falling apart. A special blend of ink is used, the contents of which we will never know. It is overprinted with symbols and then it is starched to make it water resistant and pressed to give it that nice crisp look.

If you look on the front of the bill, you will see the United States Treasury Seal. On the top you will see the scales for the balance — a balanced budget. In the center you have a carpenter's T-square, a tool used for an even cut. Underneath is the key to the United States Treasury. That's all pretty easy to figure out, but what is on the back of that dollar bill is something we should all know. If you turn the bill over, you will see two circles. Both circles, together, comprise the Great Seal of the United States. The First Continental Congress requested that Benjamin Franklin and a group of men come up with a seal. It took them four years to accomplish this task and another two years to get it approved.

If you look at the left-hand circle, you will see a pyramid. Notice the face is lighted and the western side is dark. This country was just beginning. We had not begun to explore the West or decide what we could do for Western civilization. The pyramid is un-capped, again signifying that we were not even close to being finished. Inside the capstone you have the all-seeing eye, an ancient symbol for divinity. It was Franklin's belief that one man couldn't do it alone, but a group of men, with the help of God, could do anything.

"IN GOD WE TRUST" is on this currency. The Latin above the pyramid, *ANNUIT COEPTIS*, means "He [God] has favored our undertaking." The Latin below the pyramid, *NOVUS ORDO SECLORUM*, means "a new order of the ages." At the base of the pyramid is the Roman numeral for 1776.

If you look at the right-hand circle, and check it carefully, you will learn that it is on every national cemetery in the United States. It is also on the Parade of Flags Walkway at the Bushnell, Florida, National Cemetery and is the centerpiece of most heroes' monuments. Slightly modified, it is the seal of the president of the United States and it is always visible whenever he speaks, yet no one knows what the symbols mean.

In the eagle's beak you will read *E PLURIBUS UNUM,* meaning "out of many, one." Above the eagle you have 13 stars representing the 13 original colonies. Again, we were coming together as one. Notice what the eagle holds in his talons. He holds an olive branch and arrows. This country wants peace, but we will never be afraid to fight to preserve peace.

Many veterans remember coming home to an America that didn't care. Too many never came home at all. Too many patriots have sacrificed too much to ever let these symbolic meanings fade.

# The Ten Commandments

There is one thing I would like to see happen in our schools, but it will take a great many patriotic Americans to demand its emplacement. We Bible believers must lead the way in returning to every classroom in the United States of America the following words that will give the moral guidelines far too many American youngsters are not learning:

1. Thou shalt have no other gods before me.
2. Thou shalt not take the name of the Lord thy God in vain.
3. Thou shalt not make unto thee any graven image.
4. Remember the sabbath day, to keep it Holy.
5. Honor thy father and thy mother.
6. Thou shalt not kill.
7. Thou shalt not commit adultery.
8. Thou shall not steal.
9. Thou shalt not bear false witness against thy neighbor
10. Thou shalt not covet thy neighbor's house, thou shalt not covet thy neighbor's wife, nor any thing that is thy neighbor's.

There are many in our land who think these "radical" old-fashioned concepts have no place in our public schools. I have but one question for these folks: "How well has our society fared since Ms. O'Hair got God kicked out of school?" The answer is obvious. The moral free fall and decline in decency has escalated to near light speed. As long as there are tests given in school, there will be prayer! Nobody can stop it.

Now it's time to look back, to rekindle the flames that our nation was founded upon — when our leaders were all men of God and looked to our Heavenly Father for wisdom and guidance. Even George Washington was looked upon as a man whose destiny was shaped by the very hand of God Almighty. Think about this: would you rather continue down the path we have witnessed in the years leading up to September 11, or continue the return to our "roots," those times when American children were free to stand together and recite these wonderful words:

I pledge allegiance to the flag of the United States of America. And to the republic for which it stands, one nation under God, indivisible, with liberty and justice for all.

One of my new heroes is a man named David Barton. He founded WallBuilders, Inc., a Bible-believing business whose mission is paralleled in the title of this book. My "adopted" brother told me about David's work and suggested I read some of his work. One story above all others grabbed me. It's the true story of a young George Washington, a colonel, only 23 years old, and the battle that was to become legend. The sad part is that this account of God's protective shield was never taught in our schools. The battle on the Monongahela (in Pennsylvania) was certainly

one of the most significant events of his early life. A life that literally was shielded by unseen angels of protection.

Approximately 15 years after the battle, the chief of the Indian tribe Washington had fought requested a private audience with the military man whom he, the chieftain, was assigned to kill in the battle years earlier. I will paraphrase the account of what took place:

He began to speak, telling Washington that he was the chief and ruled over his tribes, his influence extending from the Great Lakes to the far mountains. He told of traveling a very long way just to meet the young warrior of the great battle so long ago. The chief told of shouting to his braves who were marksmen of the first order to make sure their aim was perfect and true to their target, the young Col. Washington. As instructed, the Indian warriors leveled their guns and took perfect aim at the horseman now riding only feet away. The triggers were pulled, sparks igniting gun-powder, propelling lead balls which each violently found their mark, ripping through Washington's coat. One Indian warrior hit his target with perfection, not once but several times, but the rider stayed mounted. Another marksman pulled his trigger, again the bullet ripped through Washington's coat but still he rode. A third hit his mark, then a fourth and fifth, but the rider remained upright and strong. Seeing his marksmen had indeed aimed true and deadly, the chieftain vowed one day to pay homage to this white warrior who was protected by God. The chieftain recalled, "Our rifles were leveled, rifles which, but for you, knew not how to miss, but it was all in vain for a power mightier than we shielded you. I

have come to pay homage to the man who was protected from heaven, and who can never die in battle."[10]

When I first heard of "The Bullet-Proof Washington," I thought the Indians had missed their mark. But in recounting the incident years later, President Washington verified the facts, telling astonished listeners that he indeed had several bullet holes that penetrated the chest of his coat, but not a bruise could be found. What is amazing is that both the Indian warriors and their intended victim told the same story. I believe George Washington was protected from on high. It's obvious God had big plans for him. This story has been authenticated by historians from both the Native Americans and scholars from leading institutions. My question is, "Why hasn't this story been taught in schools?" Aren't we still "One Nation under God?"

History proves that this "One Nation under God" was indeed founded as a Christian nation. Today, liberals in the news media would like you to believe otherwise. There is just too much proof to dispute the facts, period. But truth will prevail because there is a rebirth of patriotism in every corner of the United States. I meet thousands of wonderful, believing people who share a passion for truth, justice, and the American way of life. The momentum has begun to build and you can begin to speak out for what is right . . . because it is! Many try to say this is not a nation of Christian principles. Here is the proof that you will never see on the nightly news or read about in the newspapers because they don't want you to know about it.

In 1775, only a year after the British had invaded the colonies, the United States Congress convened to select one of its own members to organize all the farmers and militia groups into an army that would go up

against the mightiest military force on earth. No one thought we could win a war with Great Britain, but they all pledged their lives, their fortunes, and their sacred honor. George Washington said on July 9, 1776, "Every officer and man will endeavor so as to live and act as becomes a Christian soldier, defending the dearest rights and liberties of his country. To the extraordinary character of patriot, it should be our highest glory to add the more distinguished character of Christian."

These were the words of our first president who believed in his Lord's guidance and protection, whose divine protection was evident as Indian marksmen clearly proved when bullets ripped through the young Washington's coat, all failing to penetrate or even bruise the skin. Yes, Washington's words to his troops prove Christian character was paramount in his leadership and example. His directives were closely reminiscent of the orders given to the minutemen by the Provential Congress in 1774. Congress reminded the minutemen that:

> You are placed by Providence in the post of honor, because it is the post of danger. And while struggling for the noblest objectives — the liberties of your country, the happiness of posterity and the rights of human nature — the eyes not only of North America and the whole British Empire, but of all Europe are upon you. Let us be, therefore, altogether solicitous that no disorderly behavior, nothing unbecoming our characters as Americans; as citizens and Christians, be justly chargeable to us.

It is obvious our republic was indeed founded as a Christian nation. It's time we stand up and acknowledge this fact, be proud of it, share it with those around us, and defend our heritage whenever somebody tries to say otherwise. Many people have asked me, "Do you think people really care about a rebirth of patriotism?" Yes, I do think so, and I'll tell you why. People are hungry for it, and I first wrote about this nearly two years before the attacks in New York. We who served are sick and tired of those who didn't always telling us what's wrong with our country! And guess what? THEY are what's wrong with America right now. In my show in Branson I saw thousands of veterans every month and they always told me how they wished their grandkids could grow up feeling the pride we felt when we were young and it was "cool" to be proud of our flag, our nation, and our president.

Can we have a successful rebirth of patriotism in America? The reality is yes, and no. If we do nothing, say nothing, and continue to sit on our hands, I believe our great nation is doomed, because history proves once a nation abandons God, evil enters and immediately erodes the moral foundation of the society. When it collapses, so does the nation. History proves that to be true. But if enough believers will passionately stand up for God, family, and country, we will renew our spirits and pass along the legacy of good triumphing over evil. Yes, if we shout loud and clear our patriotic beliefs, people will come to join our noble cause. When millions "log-on" to the truth, truth prevails.

In the movie *Field of Dreams*, I remember when Costner's character asked James Earl Jones "IF" people would come to see his baseball field in the middle of Iowa? Jones's character smiled broadly, and with the joyful passion he felt for the game replied, "Oh, yes, people will come. They'll come for reasons they can't even fathom. They will turn in your driveway not knowing for sure why they are doing it. They'll arrive at your door as innocent as children, longing for the past. They will sit in seats and watch. It will be as if they dipped themselves in magic waters.

The memories will be so thick they'll have to brush them away from their faces. People will come. This game is part of our past. It reminds us of all that once was good and could be again. People will come. People will most definitely come."[11]

It took faith to build that baseball diamond in the middle of an Iowa cornfield. And if you saw the movie, you'll remember that he did it while his friends, family, and community thought he was crazy. Well, maybe it's time you and I act a little crazy. Let's start the tide growing by doing simple "baby steps" to renew our patriotic hearts.

*Audiences sit "up close and personal" at Mike's Remember When Theatre.*

# "Bill of No Rights"

The following has been attributed to State Representative Mitchell Kaye, Georgia.

We, the sensible people of the United States, in an attempt to help everyone get along, restore some semblance of justice, avoid any more riots, keep our nation safe, promote positive behavior, and secure the blessings of debt-free liberty to ourselves and our great-great-great-grandchildren, hereby try one more time to ordain and establish some common sense guidelines for the terminally whiny, guilt-ridden, and delusional. We hold these truths to be self-evident: that a whole lot of people are confused by the Bill of Rights and are so dim that they require a Bill of No Rights.

ARTICLE I: You do not have the right to a new car, big screen TV or any other form of wealth.

ARTICLE II: You do not have the right to never be offended. This country is based on freedom, and that means freedom for everyone — not just you! You may leave the room, turn the channel, express a different opinion, etc., but the world is full of idiots, and probably always will be. And like the rest of us, you need to simply deal with it.

ARTICLE III: You do not have the right to be free from harm. If you stick a screwdriver in your eye, learn to be more careful, do not expect the tool manufacturer to make you and all your relatives independently wealthy.

ARTICLE IV: You do not have the right to free food and housing. Americans are the most charitable people to be found, and will gladly help anyone in need, but we are quickly growing weary of subsidizing generation after generation of professional couch potatoes who achieve nothing more than the creation of another generation of professional couch potatoes.

ARTICLE V: You do not have the right to free health care. That would be nice, but from the looks of public housing, we're just not interested in health care.

ARTICLE VI: You do not have the right to physically harm other people. If you kidnap, rape, intentionally maim, or kill someone, don't be surprised if the rest of us want to see you fry in the electric chair.

ARTICLE VII: You do not have the right to the possessions of others. If you rob, cheat, or coerce away the goods or services of other citizens, don't be surprised if the rest of us get together and lock you away in a place where you still won't have the right to a big screen color TV, pool tables, weight rooms, or a life of leisure.

ARTICLE VIII: You don't have the right to a job. All of us sure want you to have a job, and will gladly help you along in hard times, but we expect you to take advantage of the opportunities of part time jobs, education, and vocational training.

ARTICLE IX: You do not have the right to happiness. Being an American means that you have the right to PURSUE happiness

— which by the way, is a lot easier if you are unencumbered by an overabundance of idiotic laws created by those of you who were confused by the Bill of Rights.

ARTICLE X: This is an English-speaking country. We don't care where you are from. We welcome you here. English is our language and, like the one you left behind, we also have a culture. Learn it or go back to the country and the living conditions you were fleeing.

Footnote: As we ponder the above, it becomes very obvious that the one thing that could alter America's destiny would be an infusion of old-fashioned "common sense." There are days I am sure you lay down for the night and ponder the madness. Remember when a handshake was called a contract? Bring back common sense!

# A Few Remember Whens . . .

Don't you wish you could go back to the time when . . .

1. Decisions were made by going "eeny-meeny-miney-mo."
2. Mistakes were corrected by simply exclaiming, "Do over!"
3. "Race issue" meant arguing about who ran the fastest.
4. Money issues were handled by whoever was the banker in "Monopoly."
5. Catching fireflies happily occupied an entire evening.
6. It wasn't odd to have two or three "best" friends.
7. Being old referred to anyone over 20.
8. The net on a tennis court was the perfect height to play volleyball, and rules didn't matter.
9. The worst thing you could catch from the opposite sex was cooties.
10. It was magic when Dad would "remove" his thumb.
11. It was unbelievable that dodge ball wasn't an Olympic event.
12. Having a weapon in school meant being caught with a slingshot.
13. Nobody was prettier than Mom.

14. Dad was the strongest man alive.

15. Scrapes and bruises were kissed and made better.

16. It was a big deal to be tall enough for the "big people" rides at the amusement park.

17. Getting a foot of snow was a dream come true.

18. Abilities were discovered because of a "double-dog" dare.

19. Saturday morning cartoons weren't 30-minute ads for action figures.

20. "Olly-olly-oxen-free" made perfect sense.

21. Spinning around, getting dizzy, and falling down was cause for giggles.

22. The worst embarrassment was being picked last for a team.

23. "War" was a card game.

24. Water balloons were the ultimate weapon.

25. Baseball cards in the spokes transformed any bike into motorcycles.

26. Taking drugs meant orange-flavored chewable Flintstone's vitamins.

27. Ice cream was considered a basic food group.

28. Older siblings were the worst tormentors, but also the fiercest protectors.

*I'd like to add a personal thought about baseball:*

29. Remember when we played baseball from sunrise to sunset? I'd shout, "I'm Mickey Mantle!" My pals would say, "I'm Willie Mays!" or "I'm Hank Aaron!" When you're a kid you don't notice the color of your hero's skin.

# I Remember When . . .

There was a time back in the early '60s when I had to work weekends at my parents' corner grocery store. The '60s was one of the most dangerous times in our nation's history. The Vietnam war claimed its victims, and we watched our televisions reporting the daily casualty counts. I was about 14 years old when all this began to happen. Race riots were flaring all across the land and it seemed our nation was falling apart at the seams. But when you are a kid, skin color doesn't seem to matter much. Here's a true story that happened one Saturday morning when I was about 16 years old.

My family owned a little grocery store in Oak Park, a section of Sacramento that was evolving into a mostly black community.

Like most teenagers, I didn't like working all that much. My stepfather, Gerald Radford, is an honest, hardworking man who felt if you didn't work hard, high achievement was impossible. "Hard work never hurt anybody!" he always said. So, reluctantly, each Saturday morning, as was my assignment, I'd punch the keys on the old cash register at Radford's Market.

One particular Saturday morning a bouncy, happy little black girl came skipping her way up to the checkout counter. "Hi, Mikey," she said. I don't remember her name, but I do remember how cute her pigtails were. It looked like she'd received an electrical shock because they were sticking straight out from both sides of her head.

"What can I get you?" I asked.

"Well, my mommy sent me down here to get some film for her camera cuz weez havin' a party today!" I could tell she was excited about it because she was aglow with anticipation.

I got down on one knee and looked into her big brown eyes and asked, "Do you need black and white film, or do you need colored?"

She scratched her head, with a puzzled look on her face. Then, with the sweetest innocence I've ever seen, replied, "Well Mikey, I don't think no white folks is comin' to da party, soze you can just give me the colored film!"

That little girl touched my heart that day. Oh, I wish the rest of us "adults" could be so blind to the color of a person's skin. The world would surely be a friendlier place.

# "If I Were the Devil"

by Paul Harvey

I would gain control of the most powerful nation in the world;
I would delude their minds into thinking that they had come from man's effort, instead of God's blessings;

I would promote an attitude of loving things and using people, instead of the other way around;

I would dupe entire states into relying on gambling for their state revenue;

I would convince people that character is not an issue when it comes to leadership;

I would make it legal to take the life of unborn babies;

I would make it socially acceptable to take one's own life, and invent machines to make it convenient;

I would cheapen human life as much as possible so that the lives of animals are valued more than human beings;

I would take God out of the schools, where even the mention of His name can bring a lawsuit;

I would come up with drugs that sedate the mind and target the young, and I would get sports heroes to advertise them.

I would get control of the media, so that every night I could pollute the minds of every family member for my agenda;

I would attack the family, the backbone of any nation. I would make divorce acceptable and easy, even fashionable. If the family crumbles, so does the nation;

I would compel people to express their most depraved fantasies on canvas and movie screens, and I would call it art;

I would convince the world that people are born homosexuals, and that their lifestyles should be accepted and marveled;

I would convince the people that right and wrong are determined by a few who call themselves authorities and refer to their agendas as politically correct;

I would persuade people that the church is irrelevant and out of date, the Bible is for the naive;

I would dull the minds of Christians, and make them believe that prayer is not important, and that faithfulness and obedience are optional.

I GUESS I WOULD LEAVE THINGS PRETTY MUCH THE WAY THEY ARE.

*Paul Harvey*

## Passing Through

### by Senator Zell Miller (D-GA)

Just like Daniel Boone passed through Cumberland Gap and opened up a new frontier, so America can pass through the Values Gap and discover something about our fellow countrymen we haven't known. And in doing so, we may even discover something about ourselves.

When I reached my 70th birthday in 2002, each of my four grand-children gave me a present. I gave them this in return:

### Some Lessons Learned by Seventy

1. Don't be afraid to fail while going after something you really, really want. You will always learn from it. NEVER GIVE UP. Persistence will overcome everything else. I guarantee it.

2. If you listen more than you talk, you will not only learn more, but people will think you're smarter, not dumb.

3. Take what you want. Take it and pay for it. You can have whatever you want, but it's going to cost you in some way — something. For every action there is a consequence — always! It may be a good consequence or a bad one, but it will come just as sure as night follows the day.

4. Use frequently but sincerely the words "I'm sorry," "thank you," and "I love you."

5. Being on time will be noted and will impress people. Being late is a rude thing to do. It says to the other people, "My time is more important than your time." A person who is always late is a selfish person.

6. Being mentally tough will help you more in life than being physically tough. They don't always go together.

7. People don't like to be around whiners. Don't be one. Ask yourself from time to time, "Am I whining too much?" Blaming others for your own misfortune is the same thing and just as bad.

8. Notice and appreciate what makes you happy. Maybe it's a song or a poem or a movie or an event or location. Maybe it's seeing, hearing, or reading something special. If nothing does this for you, examine your life, because something is missing. Man does not live by bread alone.

9. Search for your own special niche. This may take years to find although often it occurs early in life. There is something out there that you can do better or easier than most people. You just seem to have a talent for it. Find it. It's there. And when you do, others will beat a path to your door to get you to do it for them. It may bring you fame, fortune, or happiness. Keep in mind that there are also things you simply can't do very well, but there are others who can. If you're lucky, you'll marry one.

10. From time to time, make yourself do something you don't really want to do. It will make you stronger.

11. Family and home are very important. Honor them. One should know where one comes from and who sacrificed to get us where we are. Having a sense of family and having a sense of place is going to be increasingly hard to have in this modern, fast-moving, ever-changing world, but if you can have it, it will bring you much comfort and stability.

12. Keep a good sense of humor and laugh at yourself more than you do at others.

# Meeting President Reagan

One of the things that I am most devoted to is getting prayer back in schools. That one component in our children's school day would do so much to transform our nation back to the era when a child's innocence wasn't lost so early in life.

At our Remember When Theatre in Branson, I took an occasional "pulse of America," because I wanted to know what's on people's minds. Believe me, people aren't shy when asked to share their opinions about the state of our nation. Before I get ahead of myself, you need to know I recently had a chat with a radio personality on a Springfield, Missouri, "talk station." I asked him what he'd like me to talk about when he interviewed me on the show. "Your days in the Reagan White House!" He quickly added, "Tell me Mr. Reagan was as great as we all thought he was." And so began a dialogue about whom I consider not just a great communicator, but the man whose legacy created the great economy we all enjoy today. He was also the man most responsible for bringing an end to the "Evil Empire."

The year was 1981 and I had just accepted an appointment as a special advisor to the President's Council on Physical Fitness and Sports. The chairman was the late George Allen. Everyone remembers him as the head coach of the Washington Redskins, a man who took the "Over the

Hill Gang" to the Superbowl in '72. Coach Allen was known as a man of amazing energy and for doing things on a minute's notice. George called me one night about 9 o'clock and asked if I'd like to go to Washington to meet with the president. "You bet!" I nearly shouted into the phone. Two hours later we boarded a DC 10 at LAX and took the "Red Eye" midnight flight to our nation's capital.

Arriving at National Airport, now proudly known as Ronald Reagan National Airport, we were met by limo and whisked across town. Arriving at the guard gate, the driver lowered his window. The White House guard recognized him, saluting smartly as the gates electronically swung open. Rounding the driveway we have seen a thousand times on TV, we pulled under the pillars where another soldier stepped forward and opened the door. He immediately recognized George, then snapped to attention, "Welcome back, Coach."

I was in awe. It was hard to believe that I was walking inside the White House and in a few minutes would be sitting in a private meeting with our president. Mr. Reagan was the warmest and most charismatic person I've ever met. He made me feel like we were old friends. "Hi, Mike," he said. Just the fact that he knew my name was overwhelming. I must make this very clear — the president knew me because I was a friend of his friend, Coach Allen. Nevertheless, just being in the same room with him was inspiring. There was an aura about him, a true magnetism that drew you in . . . just about everyone who ever met him would tell you the same thing — he was magnetic and a true gentleman.

In the years since, I reminisce back to the last time I saw Mr. Reagan. The New York Mets had just won the World Series and Coach Allen and I stood as they presented the president with his official Mets jacket.

It was one of those crisp fall days in Washington. The leaves had turned into a rainbow of color, and the atmosphere around the White House was very cheerful. As the festivities in the Rose Garden ended, President Reagan thanked everyone for coming and walked down the sunlit hallway. Suddenly he turned and waved toward George and me. The famous smile and natural nod of his head acknowledged us in friendly recognition. That smile is what I most remember, his magnetic smile punctuated with his rosy cheeks. America will never see the likes of him again. He was truly an honored and respected gentleman. His respect for the Oval Office was so profound he would never remove his jacket. To do so, in his opinion, would dishonor the office he pledged to uphold.

This great land needs his kind again. And recent events have proven to many that President George W. Bush has "the right stuff" to lead us through the terrorist crisis. America is also in a moral crisis, but it's not too late to change our course. We must return to the old-fashioned values in which our founders believed: God, family, and country. We need men of honor such as Jefferson, Washington and Abraham Lincoln, men who believed in following the Ten Commandments.

In evaluating political candidates, I use this simple method in deciding which person gets my vote — do they believe in the Ten Commandments? All you have to do is a little homework to see how they voted on certain issues. If their voting record violates the law of any of the Commandments, they do not get my vote.

# SECTION SIX

*Great Americans —*
*In Their Words. . . .*

## George Washington

First Inaugural Address — April 30, 1789

Such being the impressions under which I have, in obedience to the public summons, repaired to the present station, it would be peculiarly improper to omit in this first official act my fervent supplications to that Almighty Being who rules over the universe, who presides in the councils of nations, and whose providential aids can supply every human defect, that His benediction may consecrate to the liberties and happiness of the people of the United States a Government instituted by themselves for these essential purposes, and may enable every instrument employed in its administration to execute with success the functions allotted to his charge. In tendering this homage to the Great Author of every public and private good, I assure myself that it expresses your sentiments not less than my own, nor those of my fellow citizens at large less than either. No people can be bound to acknowledge and adore the Invisible Hand which conducts the affairs of men more than those of the United States. Every step by which they have advanced to the character of an independent nation seems to have been distinguished by some token of providential agency; and in the important revolution just accomplished in the system of their united government the tranquil deliberations and voluntary consent of so many distinct communities from which the event has resulted cannot be compared with the means by which most governments have been established without some return of pious gratitude, along with an humble anticipation of the future blessings which the past seem to presage. These reflections, arising out of the present crisis, have forced themselves too strongly on my mind to be suppressed. You will join with me, I trust, in thinking that there are none under the influence of which the proceedings of a new and free government can more auspiciously commence.

Having thus imparted to you my sentiments as they have been awakened by the occasion which brings us together, I shall take my present leave; but not without resorting once more to the benign Parent of the Human Race in humble supplication that, since He has been pleased to favor the American people with opportunities for deliberating in perfect tranquillity, and dispositions for deciding with unparalleled unanimity on a form of government for the security of their union and the advancement of their happiness, so His divine blessing may be equally conspicuous in the enlarged views, the temperate consultations, and the wise measures on which the success of this Government depend.

*Abraham Lincoln*

The Gettysburg Address — November 19, 1863

Four score and seven years ago, our fathers brought forth upon this continent, a new nation, conceived in liberty, and dedicated to the proposition that all men are created equal.

"Now we are engaged in a great civil war, testing whether that nation or any nation so conceived and so dedicated, can long endure. We are met on a great battlefield of that war. We have come to dedicate a portion of that field, as a final resting-place for those who here gave their lives that that nation might live. It is altogether fitting and proper that we should do this. "But, in a larger sense, we cannot dedicate — we cannot consecrate — we cannot hallow — this ground. The brave men, living and dead, who struggled here, have consecrated it, far above our poor power to add or detract. The world will little neither note, nor long remember what we say here, but it can never forget what they did here. It is for

us the living, rather, to be dedicated here to the unfinished work which they who fought here have thus far so nobly advanced. It is rather for us to be here dedicated to the great task remaining before us — that from these honored dead we take increased devotion to that cause for which they gave the last full measure of devotion — that we here highly resolve that these dead shall not have died in vain — that this nation, under God, shall have a new birth of freedom — and that government of the people, by the people, for the people, shall not perish from the earth.

## Franklin D. Roosevelt

From "The Four Freedoms"

State of the Union Address — January 6, 1941

A good society is able to face schemes of world domination and foreign revolutions alike without fear. Since the beginning of our American history we have been engaged in change, in a perpetual, peaceful revolution, a revolution which goes on steadily, quietly, adjusting itself to changing conditions without the concentration camp or the quicklime in the ditch. The world order, which we seek, is the cooperation of free countries, working together in a friendly, civilized society. This nation has placed its destiny in the hands, heads, and hearts of its millions of free men and women, and its faith in freedom under the guidance of God. Freedom means the supremacy of human rights everywhere. Our support goes to those who struggle to gain those rights and keep them. Our strength is our unity of purpose. To that high concept there can be no end, save victory.

Photo courtesy of U.S. Dept. of Trans., Maritime Administration

# Harry S. Truman

## From Inaugural Address — January 20, 1949

Mr. Vice President, Mr. Chief Justice, and fellow citizens, I accept with humility the honor the American people have conferred upon me. I accept it with a deep resolve to do all that I can for the welfare of this nation and for the peace of the world.

In performing the duties of my office, I need the help and prayers of every one of you. I ask for your encouragement and your support. The tasks we face are difficult, and we can accomplish them only if we work together.

Each period of our national history has had its special challenges. Those that confront us now are as momentous as any in the past. Today marks the beginning not only of a new administration, but of a period that will be eventful, perhaps decisive, for us and for the world. It may be our lot to experience, and in large measure to bring about, a major turning point in the long history of the human race. The first half of this century has been marked by unprecedented and brutal attacks on the rights of man, and by the two most frightful wars in history. The supreme need of our time is for men to learn to live together in peace and harmony. The peoples of the earth face the future with grave uncertainty, composed almost equally of great hopes and great fears. In this

time of doubt, they look to the United States as never before for good will, strength, and wise leadership.

It is fitting, therefore, that we take this occasion to proclaim to the world the essential principles of the faith by which we live, and to declare our aims to all peoples.

The American people stand firm in the faith which has inspired this nation from the beginning. We believe that all men have a right to equal justice under law and equal opportunity to share in the common good. We believe that all men have the right to freedom of thought and expression. We believe that all men are created equal because they are created in the image of God. From this faith we will not be moved.

# Dwight D. Eisenhower

From Inaugural Address — January 20, 1953

My friends, before I begin the expression of those thoughts that I deem appropriate to this moment, would you permit me the privilege of uttering a little private prayer of my own. And I ask that you bow your heads: Almighty God, as we stand here at this moment, my future associates in the executive branch of government join me in beseeching that Thou will make full and complete our dedication to the service of the people in this throng, and their fellow citizens everywhere. Give us, we pray, the power to discern clearly right from wrong, and allow all our words and actions to be governed thereby, and by the laws of this land. Especially we pray that our concern shall be for all the people regardless of station, race, or calling. May cooperation be permitted and be the mutual aim of those who, under the concepts of our Constitution, hold to differing political faiths; so that all may work for the good of our beloved country and Thy glory. Amen.

Patriotism means equipped forces and a prepared citizenry. Moral stamina means more energy and more productivity, on the farm and in the factory. Love of liberty means the guarding of every resource that makes freedom possible, from the sanctity of our families and the wealth of our soil to the genius of our scientists. And so each citizen plays an indispensable role. The productivity of our heads, our hands, and our hearts is the source of all the strength we can command, for both the enrichment of our lives and the winning of the peace. No person, no home, no community can be beyond the reach of this call. We are summoned to act in wisdom and in conscience, to work with industry, to teach with persuasion, to preach with conviction, to weigh our every deed with care and with compassion. For this truth must be clear before us: whatever America hopes to bring to pass in the world must first come to pass in the heart of America. The peace we seek, then, is nothing less than the practice and fulfillment of our whole faith among ourselves and in our dealings with others. This signifies more than the stilling of guns, easing the sorrow of war. More than escape from death, it is a way of life. More than a haven for the weary, it is a hope for the brave. This is the hope that beckons us onward in this century of trial. This is the work that awaits us all, to be done with bravery, with charity, and with prayer to Almighty God.

# *John F. Kennedy*

From Inaugural Address — January 20, 1961

We observe today not a victory of party, but a celebration of freedom — symbolizing an end, as well as a beginning — signifying renewal, as well as change. For I have sworn before you and Almighty God the same solemn oath our forebearers prescribed nearly a century and three quarters ago. The world is very different now. For man holds in his mortal hands the power to abolish all forms of human poverty and all forms of human life. And yet the same revolutionary beliefs for which our forebears fought are still at issue around the globe, the belief that the rights of man come not from the generosity of the state, but from the hand of God. We dare not forget today that we are the heirs of that first revolution.

Let the word go forth from this time and place, to friend and foe alike, that the torch has been passed to a new generation of Americans, born in this century, tempered by war, disciplined by a

hard and bitter peace, proud of our ancient heritage, and unwilling to witness or permit the slow undoing of those human rights to which this nation has always been committed, and to which we are committed today at home and around the world.

Let every nation know, whether it wishes us well or ill, that we shall pay any price, bear any burden, meet any hardship, support any friend, oppose any foe, in order to assure the survival and the success of liberty. So let us begin anew, remembering on both sides that civility is not a sign of weakness, and sincerity is always subject to proof. Let us never negotiate out of fear. But let us never fear to negotiate.

Since this country was founded, each generation of Americans has been summoned to give testimony to its national loyalty. The graves of young Americans who answered the call to service surround the globe. Now the trumpet summons us again not as a call to bear arms, though arms we need; not as a call to battle, though embattled we are, but a call to bear the burden of a long twilight struggle, year in and year out, rejoicing in hope, patient in tribulation, a struggle against the common enemies of man: tyranny, poverty, disease, and war itself. The energy, the faith, the devotion which we bring to this endeavor will light our country and all who serve it and the glow from that fire can truly light the world. And so, my fellow Americans: ask not what your country can do for you, ask what you can do for your country.

# *Ronald Reagan*

From Inaugural Address — January 21, 1985

There are no words adequate to express my thanks for the great honor that you have bestowed on me. I will do my utmost to be deserving of your trust.

When the first president, George Washington, placed his hand upon the Bible, he stood less than a single day's journey by horseback from raw, untamed wilderness. There were four million Americans in a union of 13 states. Today we are 60 times as many in a union of 50 states. We have lighted the world with our inventions, gone to the aid of mankind wherever in the world there was a cry for help, journeyed to the moon and safely returned. So much has changed. And yet we stand together as we did two centuries ago.

When I took this oath four years ago, I did so in a time of economic stress. Voices were raised saying we had to look to our past for the greatness and glory. But we, the present-day Americans, are not given to looking backward. In this blessed land, there is always a better tomorrow. Four years ago, I spoke to you of a new beginning and we have accomplished that. But in another sense, our new beginning is a continuation of that beginning created two centuries ago when, for the first time in history, government, the people said, was not our master, it is our servant; its only power that which we the people allow it to have. That system has never failed us, but, for a time, we failed the system. We asked things of government that government was not equipped to give. We yielded authority to the national government that properly belonged to states or to local governments or to the people themselves. We allowed taxes and inflation to rob us of our earnings and savings and watched the great industrial machine that had made us the most productive people on earth slow down and the number of unemployed increase.

By 1980, we knew it was time to renew our faith, to strive with all our strength toward the ultimate in individual freedom consistent with an orderly society. We believed then and now there are no limits to growth and human progress when men and women are free to follow their dreams. And we were right to believe that. Tax rates have been reduced, inflation cut dramatically, and more people are employed than ever before in our history. We are creating a nation once again vibrant, robust, and alive. But there are many mountains yet to climb.

We will not rest until every American enjoys the fullness of free-dom, dignity, and opportunity as our birthright. It is our birthright as citizens of this great republic, and we'll meet this challenge. These will be years when Americans have restored their confidence and tradition of progress; when our values of faith, family, work, and neighborhood were restated for a modern age; when our economy was finally freed

from government's grip; when we made sincere efforts at meaningful arms reduction, rebuilding our defenses, our economy, and developing new technologies, and helped preserve peace in a troubled world; when Americans courageously supported the struggle for liberty, self-government, and free enterprise throughout the world, and turned the tide of history away from totalitarian darkness and into the warm sunlight of human freedom.

My fellow citizens, our nation is poised for greatness. We must do what we know is right and do it with all our might. Let history say of us, "These were golden years, when the American Revolution was reborn, when freedom gained new life, when America reached for her best."

# Final Words

President Reagan referred to these times as the "golden years" when the American Revolution was reborn. We sit again with a glorious opportunity before us, a time of renewal but also a time of choices that have been bestowed upon us. Do we choose to follow the path cut by Washington, Jefferson, and our founding fathers and mothers? Do we accept the challenges offered in the great speeches on the previous pages just read, or do we once again fall victim to apathy. Do we want to go back to the way it was prior to 9-11-01? Or do we want this rebirth of patriotism to continue? And please don't believe the news media! These folks are "spinning" the news to be what they want it to be.

Other critical choices are still before us. Do we want to limit government's reach into our pockets and purses, or to allow "Big Brother's" claws to dig deeper into our hides just as a monster hungers for ever more flesh? Do we, as citizens of a free and sovereign nation, wish to limit our freedoms or do we stand tall as passionate patriots and shout, "Don't tread on me!" The paths are clearly marked before us. Our future as a free society is contingent upon recognizing the expanding peril enlarging like a cancer inside the hallowed halls in Washington. There are many politicians, on both sides of the aisle, who are driven to make us slaves of an Orwellian society. Some preach words of compassion and shared responsibility, which simply means they want to take your money and give it to others. Some speak words they "hope" we believe, even though they do not. And so I ask you, do you want to control your life's destiny, or are you comfortable knowing someone else will? It could come to that if we sit by and do nothing.

However, I strongly believe we will survive the approaching crisis, both morally and ideologically. Our founding fathers pledged their lives, their fortunes, and their sacred honor because they were fed up paying the British government for taxation without representation. They indeed lived by their word and lost everything in the revolution. Do you know what the high tax rate was that sent them to war with the world's biggest power? Ap-

proximately two percent! Think about that, next April 15! I believe God will continue to bless America, IF we turn back to Him. The founders knew the power of God's word and the dynamic miracles of His hand. Their certainty and trust in His laws can be seen in every instrument of freedom they penned.

*This prophetic photograph was taken in New York City on June 29, 2000, by Ed Van Dongen. The flag, at half staff, was to honor Parks Department employees killed in a plane crash in Alaska.*

We, too, must observe God's laws, and preserve what so many gave their lives defending, because the United States of America is "one nation under God, indivisible with liberty and justice for all."

# *Preamble to the Constitution*

We, the people of the United States, in order to form a more perfect union, establish justice, insure domestic tranquility, provide for the common defense, promote the general welfare, and secure the blessings of liberty to ourselves and our posterity, do ordain and establish this Constitution for the United States of America.

# *Bill of Rights*

### (The First Ten Amendments to the Constitution of The United States of America)

### Amendment I
Congress shall make no law respecting an establishment of religion, or prohibiting the free exercise thereof; or abridging the freedom of speech, or of the press; or the right of the people peaceably to assemble, and to petition the government for a redress of grievances.

### Amendment II
A well regulated militia, being necessary to the security of a free state, the right of the people to keep and bear arms, shall not be infringed.

## Amendment III

No soldier shall, in time of peace be quartered in any house, without the consent of the owner, nor in time of war, but in a manner to be prescribed by law.

## Amendment IV

The right of the people to be secure in their persons, houses, papers, and effects, against unreasonable searches and seizures, shall not be violated, and no warrants shall issue, but upon probable cause, supported by oath or affirmation, and particularly describing the place to be searched, and the persons or things to be seized.

## Amendment V

No person shall be held to answer for a capital, or otherwise infamous crime, unless on a presentment or indictment of a grand jury, except in cases arising in the land or naval forces, or in the militia, when in actual service in time of war or public danger; nor shall any person be subject for the same offense to be twice put in jeopardy of life or limb; nor shall be compelled in any criminal case to be a witness against himself, nor be deprived of life, liberty, or property, without due process of law; nor shall private property be taken for public use, without just compensation.

## Amendment VI

In all criminal prosecutions, the accused shall enjoy the right to a speedy and public trial, by an impartial jury of the state and district wherein the crime shall have been committed, which district shall have been previously ascertained by law, and to be informed of the nature and cause of the accusation; to be confronted with the witnesses against him; to have compulsory process for obtaining witnesses in his favor, and to have the assistance of counsel for his defense.

## Amendment VII

In suits at common law, where the value in controversy shall exceed twenty dollars, the right of trial by jury shall be preserved, and no fact tried by a jury, shall be otherwise reexamined in any court of the United States, than according to the rules of the common law.

## Amendment VIII

Excessive bail shall not be required, nor excessive fines imposed, nor cruel and unusual punishments inflicted.

## Amendment IX

The enumeration in the Constitution, of certain rights, shall not be construed to deny or disparage others retained by the people.

## Amendment X

The powers not delegated to the United States by the Constitution, nor prohibited by it to the states, are reserved to the states respectively, or to the people.

# How to Properly Display the Flag of the United States

General Information:

Inauguration Day

Martin Luther King's Birthday, 3rd Monday January

Lincoln's Birthday, Feb. 12

President's Day, 3rd Monday February

Memorial Day, Last Monday May (half staff until noon)

Flag Day, June 14

Independence Day, July 4

Labor Day, 1st Monday September

Columbus Day, 2nd Monday October

Veterans Day, November 11

Election Day

Thanksgiving Day

State Holidays

All Patriotic Occasions

It is the universal custom to display the flag only from sunrise to sunset on buildings and on stationary flagstaffs in the open, but it should not be displayed on days when the weather is inclement.

If flown at night, the flag should be illuminated.

Always hoist the flag briskly, and lower it ceremoniously.

When flown at half staff, first raise to the peak, then lower to half staff. Before lowering the flag, raise it again to the peak, then lower.

If the flag becomes wet or damp, spread out the flag until dry. Do not fold or roll up when damp.

The flag, if no longer fitting for display, should be destroyed in a dignified way, preferably by burning privately.

Never should any disrespect be shown the flag of the United States of America.

The flag should never be dipped to any person or thing.

Regimental colors, state flags, and organizations or institution flags are dipped as a mark of honor.

Advertising signs should not be fastened to a staff or halyard from which the flag flies.

The flag should never be displayed with the union down except as a sign of dire distress. The flag should never touch anything beneath it or the ground, floors, water, or merchandise. Never use the flag as drapery.

Never use the flag as a covering or drape a ceiling.

The flag should never have anything placed or written upon it.

Always display the flag to the right side of any lectern or stage.

When the United States flag flies on the same halyard, no foreign flag shall be above it.

When displayed other than on a staff, it should always have the union uppermost left as seen from the wall.

When displayed over a street, the flag should be displayed with the stripes vertical, and the union to the north on an east/west street, or to the east on a north/south street.

# A Letter to God

Dear God,

Why weren't you in the schools to protect us from the evil ones who wanted to shoot us?

Signed,
A broken-hearted kid

God writes back:

Dear Broken-hearted,

Since 1962, your politicians wouldn't allow me to be in your schools anymore.

Signed,
God

PS: However, since September 11, 2001 — millions are now seeking My face and inviting Me back in schools all across America.

# *Endnotes*

## *Credit and Thanks to:*

1. Colin Powell, Secretary of State, U.S. Army General (ret.); source: Internet.
2. Sister Helen Mrosia; source: Internet.
3. Darrell Scott, transcript, Congressional Record; source: Internet.
4. Doris Haddock, transcript, Congressional Record; source: Internet.
5. Original script courtesty of Standard Broadcasting Corporation, Ltd., © 1973 by Gordon Sinclair, published by Star Quality Music (SOCAN), a Division of Unidisc Music, Inc., 578 Hymus Boulevard, Pointe-Claire, Quebec, Canada H9R 4T2.
6. Gordon Sinclair, source: Internet.
7. Nick Gholson, source: Internet.
8. Reverend Joe Wright, transcript, Kansas State Senate.
9. David C. Graham, source: Dear Abby, June 14, 1999.
10. David Barton, *The Bulletproof George Washington* (Aledo, TX: Wallbuilders Press, 1990).
11. Phil Alden Robinson, *Field of Dreams*, Universal Studios.

# About the Author
## Ambassador of Patriotism

**M**ike Radford has long been known as a passionate proponent of veterans and their families. Missouri State Rep. Sam Gaskill first labeled him "Ambassador" in 1999 — leading the effort to have Radford officially recognized in the Missouri House of Representatives and Washington, D.C. Gaskill's effort led to endorsements from every branch of the military, along with dozens of political leaders and bipartisan organizations. Gaskill, a former Air Force combat pilot during the Vietnam War, says Radford's work is vital in waking up the nation's society to the fact that veterans and their families are the real heroes. "I believe Mike is the guy who'll get things done," Gaskill said. "As an official ambassador he will motivate everyone, young and old alike, to return to the values that made our nation great."

Radford was a special advisor to the administrations of both President Reagan and President Bush Sr., working with the FBI, Justice Department, the DEA, and the President's Council on Physical Fitness and Sports. He was appointed by Senator Bob Dole's office and the WWII Memorial foundation in Washington, D.C., to spearhead Branson's fundraising efforts for the memorial. In 2001, he was given the True American Hero Award by the Retired Officers Association in Branson, Missouri. In 2003, the Congressional Medal of Honor Society presented Mike with the Bob Hope Patriot Award.

When not performing in Branson, Radford travels America speaking at air shows, conventions, military reunions, churches, and corporate events. Visit Mike at <www.mikeradford.com>.

# FRANKLIN PARK PUBLIC LIBRARY
## FRANKLIN PARK, IL.

Each borrower is held responsible for all library material drawn on his card and for fines accruing on the same. No material will be issued until such fine has been paid.

All injuries to library material beyond reasonable wear and all losses shall be made good to the satisfaction of the Librarian.

**Replacement costs will be billed after 42 days overdue.**